Modern Raw

Healthy Raw-Vegan Meals for a Balanced Life

Rachel Carr

Raw Chef and
Founder of Plant Craft

PAGE STREET
PUBLISHING CO.

PAGE STREET
PUBLISHING CO.

First published in 2019 by

Page Street Publishing Co.

27 Congress Street, Suite 105

Salem, MA 01970

www.pagestreetpublishing.com

Distributed by Macmillan, sales in Canada by The Canadian Manda Group.

23 22 21 20 19   1 2 3 4 5

ISBN-13: 978-1-62414-725-8

ISBN-10: 1-62414-725-9

Library of Congress Control Number: 2018957259

Cover and book design by Kylie Alexander for Page Street Publishing Co.

Photography by Rachel Carr

Printed and bound in the United States

Dedication

For Dawn Weisberg, my friend who inspired my raw journey with her own healing path and her love of delicious food and beauty.

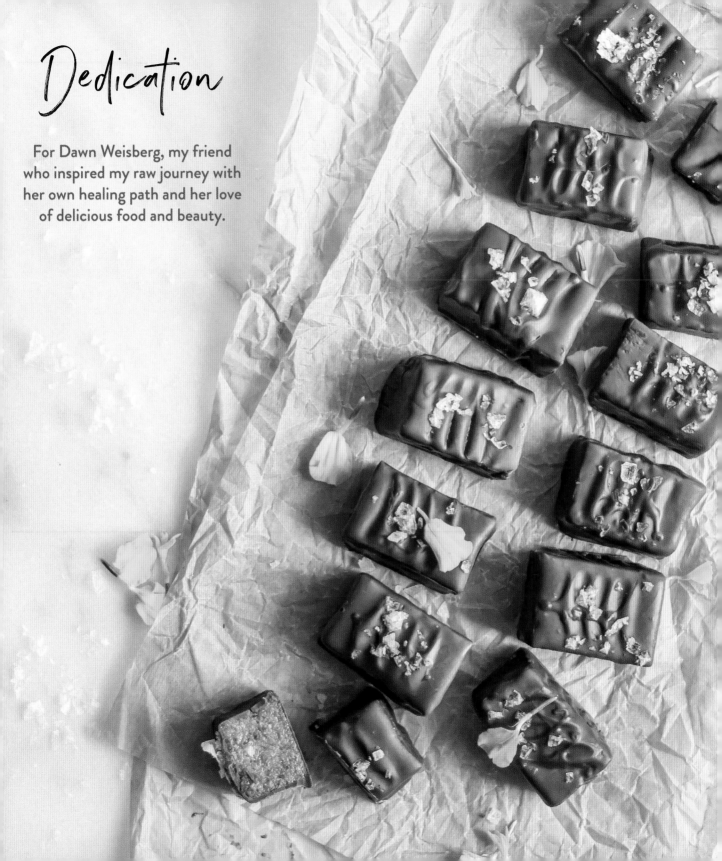

Contents

Introduction

Welcome to the vibrant, healthy and colorful world of raw and living foods. Perhaps you are new to a raw food or plant-based lifestyle and are looking for some basic information, recipes and techniques. Or maybe you have been a raw vegan for years and are interested in fresh inspiration and flavors. Whatever your background, I hope to share some delicious and healthy recipes from my many years as a raw vegan and plant-based chef.

I have been a chef for over twelve years, and I have cooked in many different styles, from Peruvian to classic American comfort food, but the cuisine that I know the best and align with personally is raw vegan.

I was introduced to raw food when a friend of mine decided to go raw to lose weight. I agreed to do it with her, to be her raw food buddy, so to speak. I thought I would just be doing it for 30 days, but as my friend and I went through the inevitable transformation, we both decided at the end of the month to commit ourselves to it completely. I loved the way I felt and also loved the freedom of being able to eat as much as I liked (and food that I loved!) and not have to worry about counting calories. It became such a passion that I decided to change careers from costume design to become a raw vegan chef to share my passion with others. I ended up, as the universe would have it, landing a job as head chef in a raw vegan restaurant called Cru, one block from my apartment at the time! I thought I would only be there for a few months, but that happy accident went on for seven years, and I have been a chef ever since!

I have since worked in many different plant-based restaurants but have never lost my love of raw food. This book will cover many recipes from my time at Cru, and some I developed later. But all the recipes in this book share the same philosophy: organic, fresh, raw produce is the star, with flavorful sauces and garnishes made from hearty, protein-rich nuts and seeds. Some of the recipes are simple and ready in five minutes, whereas others are more complex with advanced raw vegan techniques. I will cover everything from breakfast to gourmet raw vegan entrées, soups, appetizers and desserts. There is even a chapter dedicated to the type of cooked food that complements a high raw vegan lifestyle.

Before we begin getting into the nitty-gritty, I'd like to say that for me, a raw vegan diet is the simplest, most natural way to eat imaginable. It's a relief to think that when you walk into a grocery store, you can just bypass almost all of the aisles in the center and just go straight to the produce section and you're done, with a quick stop by the bulk bin for some nuts and seeds! I eventually stopped thinking of anything but raw plants as food fit to eat. There is so much more variety in the world of produce than I ever imagined before beginning this lifestyle.

In this book, I will show you the wide variety of dishes that are possible on a raw vegan diet using common equipment you may already have in your kitchen! It's possible to make a stunning raw vegan version of most of your favorite dishes—it just takes an open mind, a few basic skills and a little experimentation.

In this book, you'll find familiar favorites such as pasta (see Spaghetti and "Meatballs," page 69), pizza (see Pumpkin Seed and Cilantro Pesto Pizza, page 65) and even tacos (see Walnut-Chorizo Tacos with Kiwi Salsa and Guacamole, page 59)! There are also elegant appetizers, fresh salads and refreshing soups. And don't forget about delicious breakfast options, such as Gooey Cinnamon Rolls (page 14) and Spinach, Leek and Sun-Dried Tomato Quiche (page 25). You will have everything at your fingertips to create healthy and satisfying meals on the go or to put together stunning, elegant raw vegan dinner parties and gatherings.

First, let's define what raw food means! You might have heard such terms as raw food and living food used interchangeably. It can get a little confusing at times, but there is a subtle yet important difference. Raw foods are plant-based foods (fruits, vegetables, nuts and seeds) that are eaten either in their natural state or minimally processed, never being exposed to temperatures above 118°F (48°C). In this way, they maintain their highest and most potent nutrition content. Live or living foods are also foods that are consumed fresh, raw and/or in a condition as close as possible to their original, vibrant, living state, but can also refer to foods that have been soaked, sprouted or fermented to activate their potential life force, as in the case of sprouts.

A raw vegan diet consists entirely of fresh fruits and vegetables, nuts and seeds. Raw vegans will also sometimes use organic oils; cider vinegar, fermented foods and live cultures; spices; and limited use of certain sweeteners, such as date syrup, maple syrup or agave nectar.

A "high raw" diet describes the approach taken in this book—it means a diet containing a high percentage of raw and living foods. There are definitely some cooked foods possible in this approach!

Although some people choose to follow an exclusively raw diet, it can be difficult for certain individuals to follow. In a high raw lifestyle, eat as many fresh fruits and vegetables as possible, supplementing with nuts and seeds, and you will reap many of the benefits. A high raw diet that includes some high-quality cooked foods, gives most of the fantastic benefits of raw veganism (high nutrition content, improved digestion, easy weight management, high energy, etc.) with the flexibility of including certain cooked foods (usually ones that are minimally processed, whole foods, vegan and gluten-free).

I think it's best not to think of a high raw lifestyle as a diet, but rather as a spectrum of healthy choices you can make on your own terms. Diets don't work, and most people think of them as being something you only do for a while. I want to help you make healthier sustainable habits that stick!

But don't take my word for it! When you start to eat more raw food, you will start to experience many of the benefits yourself firsthand. As your energy and vitality return, you will find that your whole mental outlook changes and becomes as fresh, vibrant and colorful as the produce you'll naturally crave. You truly are what you eat.

When you start consuming more whole, raw plant foods, you will become your most natural, beautiful and whole self, and you are going to love the way you feel and the effects it has on your well-being. Your body will more easily find its natural weight, and you will have more energy, peace and mental clarity. You will find that your health gradually and steadily improves as you eat more pure plant foods. I have rarely experienced even as much as a cold since embracing a high raw lifestyle.

Even if you don't choose to pursue a plant-based lifestyle or raw food diet, it's a great choice to include as many raw fruits and vegetables as you can in your daily routine, in the form of salads, smoothies and juices, to boost the nutrition. Also, when cooking, try to cook vegetables very lightly until just done to preserve as much of their natural water content, fragile enzymes, vitamins and minerals as possible; however, if you choose a high raw lifestyle, all your food will be at its peak nutritional content.

Raw foods are so fresh and alive, full of juicy, unadulterated flavors as nature intended. After eating this way for a short period, you will find that there is a transformation in your taste buds. You will find yourself craving simple foods and enjoying their flavors more than ever before. Very green and even bitter flavors, such as mustard greens and collard greens, will taste healthy and nourishing. You might find you appreciate familiar foods more than ever before, as if tasting them for the first time!

After all, the secret to making great food starts with the best ingredients, no matter what eating philosophy you follow.

On a final note, I find labels such as raw foodist can contribute to stress and perfectionism, which is the last thing anyone needs! Food should be a source of joy and nourishment. Leaving behind black and white thinking about the "perfect diet" helps you deal more effectively with real challenges that arise when making any healthy change. Cravings are one of the hardest roadblocks you will face when transitioning to a high raw diet. Including high-quality, nutrient-dense, lightly cooked vegan dishes is a tasty way to stay satisfied and not fall off the wagon.

When I eat cooked food, I like it to follow these guidelines:

- light use of high temperature cooking techniques

- use of high-quality ingredients, such as organic oils, Celtic sea salt, organic tamari, etc.

- completely gluten-free

- free of processed ingredients

- completely organic, with a focus on vegetables rather than beans or grains

- use of high-quality cooking equipment—no aluminum or Teflon, only stainless steel and cast iron

It's not in the scope of this book to cover all the great reasons to adopt a plant-based lifestyle, but believe me, you won't regret it! It was the best decision I ever made, and every day, I find new ways to enjoy and celebrate all kinds of plants! My hope is that you will find new techniques, ingredients, tools and flavors to explore within the pages of this book.

Rachel Carr

Breakfast of Champions

Starting the Day Off Right

One of the questions that I get most often is, "What do you eat for breakfast on a raw vegan diet?" I try not to skip breakfast completely, as I will end up ravenously hungry. That's why it's a good idea to have some go-to recipes that you can whip up. Smoothies are one of my favorite things to grab on busy mornings (try the All Day Energy Smoothie, page 21). Sometimes, however, you might want to throw a fancy brunch for your friends and family, make something special for a holiday morning or have something a little more substantial to keep you going. Don't worry, I've got you covered!

If you're in a hurry but want more than a smoothie, try making a batch of Cranberry-Almond Power Muffins (page 26) or Brazil Nut-Chocolate Apricot Bars (page 29). These will keep for weeks in your refrigerator and contain tons of healthy fats and protein. To get a little more fancy-schmancy, whip up some Spinach, Leek and Sun-Dried Tomato Quiches (page 25) or a Coconut Yogurt Parfait (page 30).

The important thing is that you choose what is best for you and what provides your body with the fuel it needs and helps you reach your personal goals.

Gooey Cinnamon Rolls

with Cinnamon-Date Filling

Cinnamon rolls are one of those decadent treats that remind you of childhood—gooey and warm, sweet and full of spice. This raw vegan version will make that morning cup of joe taste even better, because there's no guilt! I love to eat these straight out of the dehydrator or oven, when the icing is still nice and soft on the warm rolls. These rolls are completely gluten-free! I recommend that you roll out the dough between two pieces of plastic wrap on your cutting board. The dough is very sticky.

Makes 12 rolls

Cinnamon-Date Filling

⅓ cup (78 ml) raw honey, agave nectar or pure maple syrup

1 tbsp (7 g) ground cinnamon

½ cup (76 g) raisins

½ cup (89 g) dates

Dough

1 cup (95 g) almond flour

1 cup (178 g) buckwheat groats, soaked in water for 30 minutes, then rinsed

¼ tsp salt

1 tsp ground cinnamon

¼ cup (60 ml) coconut oil

1 apple, cored, peeled and diced

⅔ cup (90 g) flax meal, plus more for rolling (see Notes)

½ cup (118 ml) water, or as needed

⅔ cup (100 g) raisins, soaked in water for 1 hour, then drained

Coconut-Vanilla Icing

½ cup (56 g) cashews, soaked in water for 2 hours, then rinsed

¾ cup (115 g) young Thai coconut meat

⅓ cup (83 ml) agave nectar

2 tbsp (30 ml) melted coconut oil

¼ tsp vanilla extract

Pinch of salt

For the cinnamon-date filling, in a blender or food processor, combine all the filling ingredients and blend until smooth.

For the dough, in a food processor, combine the almond flour, buckwheat groats, salt, cinnamon, coconut oil, apple, flax meal, water and raisins. Puree until smooth, adding the water little by little as needed to create a doughlike texture. Turn out the dough onto a cutting board that has been covered in plastic wrap and dusted with flax meal. Cover the dough with another sheet of plastic wrap and roll into a 9 x 12-inch (23 x 30.5-cm) rectangle. Remove the plastic wrap covering the top of the dough and spread the cinnamon-date filling over the dough rectangle. Carefully roll up the dough into a large cylinder, using the bottom piece of plastic wrap to help you roll it evenly and firmly. Transfer the roll to a plate and place it in your refrigerator until firm, about 2 hours.

Remove the dough from the refrigerator and slice into a dozen 1-inch (2.5-cm)-thick slices. Place on nonstick sheets or parchment paper in your dehydrator and dehydrate for 2 hours at 115°F (46°C). After 2 hours, flip and dehydrate for 2 more hours.

For the icing, blend the cashews, coconut meat, agave, coconut oil, vanilla and salt. Transfer into a pastry bag and swirl onto the finished rolls.

> *notes:* Flax meal is made by grinding whole flaxseeds in a grinder or blender. You can simply place the seeds in a dry blender and process for about 30 seconds and you will have freshly ground flax meal.
>
> If you don't have a dehydrator, never fear! You can use your oven very easily to dehydrate these cinnamon rolls. Simply set your oven to its lowest setting (around 180 to 200°F [82 to 93°C] or on warm) and leave the door cracked open to prevent condensation. Because the oven will be warmer than a dehydrator, check your rolls every hour to check their doneness and make sure they're not getting too dry.

Vanilla Chia Pudding

with Fig and Raspberry

Chia seeds are incredibly grounding and satisfying if you eat lots of fruit in the morning. Their essential fatty acids keep you energized for hours and help keep your blood sugar steady. Chia pudding is extremely flexible and can take on many different flavors: try adding turmeric, cinnamon or matcha. I have used figs and raspberries here, but feel free to use whatever fruit you have on hand.

Serves 2

1 cup (236 ml) unsweetened Cashew Milk (page 18) or other nut milk

¼ cup (30 g) chia seeds

1 tbsp (15 ml) agave nectar or maple syrup (optional)

¼ tsp vanilla extract

Pinch of salt

2 to 3 fresh figs, sliced, for garnish

½ cup (61 g) raspberries, for garnish

¼ cup (30 g) Apple-Cinnamon Buckwheat Granola (page 18), for garnish

In a glass, combine the cashew milk and chia seeds and stir. Add the agave (if using), vanilla and salt and stir again. Taste and adjust the seasoning, if desired. Allow the mixture to stand for 30 minutes to thicken. Refrigerate for 1 hour to chill, or overnight. To serve, garnish with the sliced figs, raspberries and granola.

Apple-Cinnamon Buckwheat Granola

with Cashew Milk

I keep granola on hand all the time—as a snack or as a healthy, nutritious breakfast. This raw version is a great beginner dehydrator recipe and is very low in fat. I especially enjoy this as a topping for desserts, smoothie bowls and smoothies for extra crunch and dimension.

Serves 2

Cashew Milk

¼ cup (34 g) cashews (or almonds, soaked 2 hours and rinsed for almond milk)

1 cup (236 ml) water

Apple-Cinnamon Buckwheat Granola

3 dates, pitted

½ cup plus 2 tbsp (148 ml) water, divided

1 cup (283 g) raw buckwheat groats, soaked for 2 hours, then drained and rinsed thoroughly

½ cup (68 g) seeded and chopped apple

⅓ cup (60 g) sunflower seeds, soaked in water for 2 hours, then drained and rinsed

⅓ cup (60 g) pumpkin seeds, soaked in water for 2 hours, then drained and rinsed

2 tbsp (12 g) ground flaxseeds

⅓ cup (58 g) dried cranberries

1 tbsp (15 ml) melted coconut oil

1 tsp ground cinnamon

Pinch of ground nutmeg

Pinch of salt, or more to taste

To Serve

1 cup (148 g) fresh blueberries

1 cup (166 g) hulled and sliced fresh strawberries

For the cashew milk, in a blender, combine the cashews and water and blend for about 30 seconds on high speed. Strain in a fine-mesh colander and keep refrigerated until ready to use.

For the granola, in a blender, combine the dates and ½ cup (118 ml) of the water and puree to form a slurry. Transfer to a mixing bowl. Add the soaked buckwheat groats, apple, sunflower and pumpkin seeds, flaxseeds, dried cranberries, coconut oil, cinnamon, nutmeg and the remaining 2 tablespoons (30 ml) of water. Mix well, add the salt and adjust the seasoning as desired. Add more sweetener, if necessary.

Spread the mixture onto a solid nonstick dehydrator sheet and dehydrate at 115°F (46°C), stirring once or twice throughout the dehydration time, for 10 to 12 hours, or until the granola is sticky but adhering firmly.

Store in a sealed airtight container until ready to use; this will help maintain crunch and texture. Serve with the cashew milk and fresh berries. Make sure to eat immediately after adding the nut milk, as the cereal will begin to lose its crunch.

notes: If you do not have a dehydrator, you can bake this in the oven on a parchment-lined cookie sheet for 2 to 3 hours at 200 to 250°F (93 to 121°C), making sure to check and stir periodically so it bakes evenly.

Buckwheat groats are a type of seed that are often cooked like a grain. Kasha is toasted buckwheat groats. Untoasted groats are commonly sold in the bulk section of your health food store. If you can't find them, you can substitute rolled oats or kasha.

All Day Energy Smoothie

All the flavors of American breakfast in an easy, grab-and-go smoothie! Something I like to do with smoothies is to get 16-ounce (475-ml) deli containers and pre-portion all the ingredients, except the liquids, and freeze them as a ready-to-go smoothie kit. Then, all you do is pull one out of the freezer, pop it into a blender, add the liquids and go. You can do this with green smoothies as well, and just add your fresh greens right before blending.

Serves 1

¾ cup (177 ml) filtered water

3 tbsp (15 g) rolled oats, plus more for garnish

⅛ cup (14 g) cashews, soaked in water for 1 hour, then drained and rinsed

1 banana (frozen is okay), plus a second banana, chopped, for garnish

1 date

1 tbsp (8 g) flaxseeds

¼ tsp ground cinnamon

¼ cup (38 g) hulled and chopped strawberries, for garnish

In a blender, combine the water, oats, cashews, banana, date, flaxseeds and cinnamon. Blend until smooth. Serve immediately, topped with a chopped banana, chopped strawberries and additional oats.

note: Use certified gluten-free oats if you have a gluten sensitivity, or replace them with sprouted quinoa or buckwheat.

Blueberry Açai Bowl

Açai bowls make a nice change from smoothies or cereal. Full of antioxidants and vitamin C, this one will give you energy all morning. Sometimes I like to add almond milk to the smoothie base for a richer texture, but using coconut water as I did here is a lower-calorie option. You can really pile on the toppings with smoothie bowls like this one—I like to add coconut, nuts, seeds and chia. The more toppings, the better!

Serves 1

Açai Sorbet

1 (3.5-oz [100-g]) packet açai puree (such as Sambazon smoothie packs)

½ cup (118 ml) coconut water

1 tbsp (15 ml) melted coconut oil (optional)

1 frozen banana

½ cup (70 g) frozen blueberries

Garnishes

2 to 3 fresh strawberries

⅛ cup (15 g) fresh blueberries

1 or 2 fresh figs, sliced

1 tbsp (14 g) Apple-Cinnamon Buckwheat Granola (page 18)

In a blender, blend the açai with the coconut water until smooth. Add the coconut oil, frozen banana and frozen blueberries and blend until everything is smooth. Spoon the mixture into a bowl and garnish with fresh fruit and buckwheat granola.

note You can make the bowl and keep it in your freezer for up to an hour before serving.

Spinach, Leek and Sun-Dried Tomato Quiche

with Buckwheat Flax Crust

Quiche is an elegant dish to serve for a special brunch or lunch. Try this dish with a chilled cucumber soup and a light citrusy salad for a perfectly light meal.

Makes four 4-inch (10-cm) tarts

Buckwheat Flax Crust

1 cup (180 g) raw buckwheat groats

2 tbsp (11 g) ground flaxseeds (see Note)

1 tbsp (8 g) nutritional yeast

¼ tsp salt

¼ cup (60 ml) filtered water

1 tbsp (15 ml) fresh lemon juice

1½ tsp (2 g) psyllium powder

"Egg" Custard

1 yellow summer squash

¼ cup (60 ml) water

½ cup (70 g) sunflower seeds

¼ cup (144 g) chopped onion

½ tsp salt

3 tbsp (12 g) psyllium powder

3 tbsp (26 g) nutritional yeast

2 tbsp (30 ml) fresh lemon juice

1 tbsp (17 g) miso

Pinch of freshly ground black pepper

Vegetable Filling

2 cups (60 g) baby spinach

½ cup (175 g) leek, thinly sliced

⅛ cup (7 g) sun-dried tomato

¼ tsp salt

1 tbsp (15 ml) olive oil

For the crust, soak the buckwheat groats for 1 hour and then rinse until the water runs clear. After draining, put them in a food processor and puree about 2 minutes. Add the remaining crust ingredients and process more until a smooth dough is produced. Remove from the food processor, divide dough into 4 balls and set aside while you prepare your tart pans. I used 4-inch (10-cm) tart pans with removable bottoms, which were about ¾ inch (2 cm) high.

First, line the bottom and sides of the tart pan loosely with plastic wrap. Take a ball of the dough and press it into the bottom of the pan. Take another piece of plastic wrap and drape it on top of the pan and begin to push the dough into a crust shape in the bottom of the pan and up the sides. The dough is very sticky, and I have found that using plastic wrap on top helps keep it from sticking to your hands while you shape the dough and lets you create a smooth and even crust fairly quickly. The crusts should be no thicker than ¼ inch (6 mm) or taller than 1 inch (2.5 cm). When done forming the dough, remove the top layer of plastic and use a spatula or butter knife to smooth the top edge. Finish forming all the crusts and place them in your dehydrator for 2 hours at 115°F (46°C). After 2 hours, remove the crusts from the molds and place them back in the dehydrator for another 2 hours. Remove the finished crusts from the dehydrator.

For the "egg" custard, peel and chop the summer squash into large pieces and place in a blender. Add the rest of the custard ingredients to the blender and blend until smooth and creamy. Set aside until ready to assemble the quiches.

For the vegetable filling, in a mixing bowl, combine the spinach, sliced leek and sun-dried tomato. Add the salt and olive oil and toss well until thoroughly coated. Add the custard and mix well. Divide the mixture equally among the crusts and fill each crust. Each should be filled all the way to the top as the crust will shrink after being cooked in the dehydrator. Place all the filled quiche crusts back in the dehydrator and dry at 115°F (46°C), rotating them on the tray halfway through the drying time so they dry evenly, for 2 to 4 hours, depending on how done you would like them to be.

These can be made ahead of time and either frozen or refrigerated and reheated later in the dehydrator for about 1 hour at 115°F (46°C). Serve with a salad.

> *note* To grind the flax for the crust, you can simply put it in your blender and process it for a few seconds, and it will be ground up very quickly. It's okay to have a few whole seeds here and there in the mixture.

Cranberry—Almond Power Muffins

Make a batch of these at the beginning of the week and keep them in a resealable plastic bag in your fridge so you always have something healthy to take on those busy mornings. I am not much of a breakfast person, so I love to have these as an afternoon snack. I like to play around with the fruit to change the flavor—currants and raisins work equally well.

Makes 8 to 10 muffins

1 cup (96 g) almond flour

1 cup (112 g) walnuts

1 cup (80 g) rolled oats

½ cup (118 ml) date syrup, pure maple syrup, agave nectar or brown rice syrup

1 cup (180 g) dried cranberries

3 tbsp (45 ml) smooth almond butter

2 tbsp (30 ml) melted coconut oil

1 tbsp (8 g) ground cinnamon

½ tsp vanilla extract

Pinch of sea salt

Line a muffin pan with 8 to 10 paper cupcake wrappers. Set aside.

In a food processor, combine the almond flour, walnuts and rolled oats and process until finely ground. Transfer to a mixing bowl. Add the date syrup, cranberries, almond butter, coconut oil, cinnamon, vanilla and salt. Mix well with a wooden spoon until everything is well combined and a dough is formed.

Spoon about 2 tablespoons (30 g) of the dough into the prepared cupcake papers. Push the dough into the paper until it looks like a little muffin. Continue until all the dough is used, which should make 8 to 10 muffins. Remove the muffins from the pan carefully and place on a dehydrator tray. Dehydrate for 8 to 12 hours at 118°F (48°C).

Drizzle with some of the Coconut-Vanilla Icing from the Gooey Cinnamon Rolls (page 14) if desired. Keep refrigerated for up to 2 weeks.

Brazil Nut–Chocolate Apricot Bars

If you don't have time to sit down for breakfast, grab one of these bars on your way out the door, and you'll have energy all morning long. Although you can use almost any nuts to make these bars, I love to use Brazil nuts because they are a nutrition powerhouse. Packed with selenium, Brazil nuts are known to improve your sexual performance, protect against cancer and boost your metabolism. They also help fight inflammation and are high in vitamin E, both properties that help boost the beauty of your skin. Yes, please!

Makes 6 to 8 bars

Brazil Nut–Chocolate Apricot Bars

2 cups (234 g) Brazil nuts (or you can use walnuts, pecans, pistachios, etc.)

1 cup (83 g) chopped dried apricots (unsweetened and unsulfured, if possible)

Pinch of salt

1 tsp ground cinnamon

1 tbsp (15 ml) date syrup or pure maple syrup (optional)

2 tbsp (30 ml) water

Chocolate Glaze

½ cup (55 g) raw cacao powder

½ cup (118 ml) melted coconut oil

2 to 3 tbsp (30 to 45 ml) pure maple syrup

Pinch of Himalayan pink salt

For the bars, in a food processor, pulse the Brazil nuts until they are broken up into small pieces. Add the apricots, salt and cinnamon to the processor. Pulse until the apricots are well incorporated and the mixture begins to stick together. Add the date syrup, if using, and water and pulse again. Form the mixture into bars or balls and place in your dehydrator for 2 hours at 118°F (48°C).

For the chocolate glaze, in a high-speed blender, combine all the glaze ingredients and blend until creamy smooth and slightly warm. Drizzle the glaze on top of the bars, then allow to set in your refrigerator until hardened, 1 hour.

note If you use the chocolate glaze, keep these bars refrigerated, as the glaze is a little sticky.

Coconut Yogurt Parfait

with Nuts, Seeds and Fresh Berries

Try this coconut yogurt as a substitute for whipped cream on vegan desserts or as a yogurt in the mornings. The creamy texture and healthy fats stand in for dairy so well. Try building a few of these in mason jars to have a healthy snack ready to take on the go.

Serves 2

Coconut Yogurt

1½ cups (376 g) young Thai coconut meat (from 2 or 3 coconuts—see Note)

¼ cup (60 ml) cider vinegar

2 tbsp (30 ml) water

2 tbsp (30 ml) agave nectar (optional)

2 tbsp (30 ml) melted coconut oil

Parfait Layers

1 tbsp (9 g) raw almonds, chopped

1 tbsp (10 g) hemp seeds

1 tbsp (4 g) raw pumpkin seeds

¼ cup (40 g) fresh strawberries, sliced

¼ cup (40 g) fresh blueberries

¼ cup (30 g) raspberries

For the coconut yogurt, in a high-powered blender, combine the coconut meat, vinegar, water, agave (if using) and coconut oil and blend until smooth. The agave is completely optional—it sweetens it a little more, but honestly, the coconut meat is pleasantly sweet on its own. Transfer the mixture to a container and place it in the refrigerator to chill. When ready to serve, layer 1 cup (236 ml) of the coconut yogurt with the nuts, seeds and mixed fresh fruit. Store the remaining coconut yogurt in the refrigerator to enjoy separately.

note For the young Thai coconut meat, you will be opening fresh coconuts—the pointy white ones with fresh coconut juice, not the hairy brown ones. There are plenty of videos online about how to open one safely, so I will not bore you with that! Be sure to save the fresh coconut juice for smoothies or to enjoy just by itself. If the meat is purple/pink or too jellylike to use, you may need to try another coconut. Unfortunately, it's very hard to tell from the outside how the meat is on the inside—so buy an extra if you can. They will keep in the refrigerator for at least a week unopened. Don't throw away the juice! It's delicious!

Upgrading Dinner

Raw Vegan Classic Entrées

If you've never tried your hand at preparing raw vegan entrées, get ready to be wowed! You will be amazed by how well you can re-create familiar flavors and textures. You will not have to live without such dishes as pasta, lasagna, fried rice and pad thai. Even pizza is on the menu!

Explore your inner chef with new ingredients, techniques and recipes. Dinner is an especially great time to get creative as you are challenged to transform your favorite dishes to raw vegan. You deserve the satisfying experience of sitting down to a substantial, mouthwatering and nourishing meal, such as raw vegan sushi, a big fat wrap or a bowl of vegetable noodles with an amazing sauce. Hardly rabbit food. My hope is that you will find a few recipes in this chapter to add some variety to your daily routine.

Zucchini Lasagna

Layered dishes like lasagna make a stunning presentation perfect for entertaining but are actually quite easy and fast to make. This version of lasagna is simply made with a hearty cashew ricotta layered with fresh basil, sliced zucchini and tomato, plus a raw tomato sauce for a genuine Italian flavor. It just takes a few minutes to throw together if you have your sauce and cheese prepped in advance. Sometimes I like to add marinated kale and mushrooms to the dish in the wintertime, but you can stick with tomatoes and zucchini in the summer when they are at their seasonal best.

Serves 2 to 4

Marinara Sauce
1½ medium vine-ripe tomatoes

1 tbsp (15 ml) olive oil

¼ tsp salt

Pinch of freshly ground black pepper

1½ tsp (4 g) nutritional yeast

⅛ tsp garlic powder

⅛ tsp onion powder

1½ tsp (2 g) chopped fresh parsley

½ sun-dried tomato

Raw Lasagna
1 medium zucchini, washed and sliced lengthwise

2 medium tomatoes, sliced into ¼" (6-mm)-thick slices

1 cup (248 g) Cashew Ricotta (page 61)

1 cup (24 g) fresh basil leaves, washed and stemmed, plus more for garnish

1 cup (178 g) cherry tomatoes, sliced

2 tbsp (16 g) nutritional yeast, for garnish (optional)

Extra virgin olive oil, for garnish (optional)

To make the marinara sauce, wash and seed the vine-ripe tomatoes, chop them roughly and place in a food processor. Pulse until a chunky sauce is formed. Add the rest of the sauce ingredients and pulse a few more times. Set aside until ready to use.

For the lasagna, wash and slice the zucchini lengthwise either on a mandoline slicer or very carefully by hand to make sure the slices are even thickness, less than ¼ inch (6 mm). Cut them into 4-inch (10-cm) lengths. Then, slice the tomatoes into ¼-inch (6-mm)-thick slices and set aside.

To build the lasagna, lay down 2 slices of the zucchini side by side on a plate. Spread some of the cashew ricotta onto the prepared zucchini slices. Top with some basil, sliced tomatoes and marinara. Lay another layer of zucchini on top and repeat with more cashew ricotta, basil, tomato slices and marinara. Top with a final layer of zucchini, marinara and some cherry tomatoes. Garnish with some pretty pieces of fresh basil and a sprinkle of nutritional yeast, if using. Drizzle with olive oil, if desired.

note This dish should be served very soon after assembling, as it will start to get runny if left to sit for any length of time. Instead, try making the individual components ahead of time and building the lasagna right before serving.

Cheesy Kelp Noodles

Just like a mac 'n' cheese, this dish is filling, comforting and great for a quick, easy lunch or dinner. If you have never had kelp noodles, you are in for a treat. They are made from the inner core of ocean kelp and are considered a raw food. They do have an unusual, rubbery appearance and crunchy texture when first taken out of the bag, but quickly soften up beautifully in the sauce of your choice. They are my favorite replacement for pasta, and you can even warm the sauce slightly to mimic the experience of cooked pasta even more.

Serves 2

1 (12-oz [340-g]) package kelp noodles

1 cup (236 ml) Nacho Cheese (page 101)

1 pt (178 g) cherry tomatoes, sliced, for garnish

1 tbsp (8 g) nutritional yeast, for garnish

Salt and freshly ground black pepper

In a colander, rinse the kelp noodles under cold water. Transfer the noodles to a mixing bowl and add the nacho cheese. Massage the cheese into the noodles well for 2 to 3 minutes and allow them to sit for 15 minutes. The noodles should soften significantly with a little time in the cheese. If you would like to warm the cheese a little, it will not only be delicious but will soften the noodles more quickly.

Portion into 2 bowls, and top with chopped cherry tomatoes, nutritional yeast and salt and pepper.

note Kelp noodles are available at many health food stores and some Asian markets in the refrigerated section. They even come in flavors, such as green tea!

Raw Wok Vegetable "Stir-Fry" Noodles

This dish couldn't be easier or more satisfying. It's a healthy version of stir-fried noodles that takes about five minutes to throw together. Scented with ginger and sesame, this dish will be delicious even the next day. I sometimes like to add seaweed and kimchi to give it extra flavor and a health boost.

Serves 2

2 zucchini, cut into noodles with a spiral slicer (see Note)

2 carrots, julienned

¼ cup (17 g) shredded red cabbage

3 shiitake mushrooms, thinly sliced

2 asparagus stalks, washed and shaved lengthwise

1 tsp peeled and grated fresh ginger

1 tsp toasted sesame oil, or more to taste

2 tbsp (30 ml) gluten-free tamari

Juice of 1 lime

Salt and freshly ground black pepper

1 tbsp (4 g) sesame seeds, for garnish

2 scallions, chopped

In a mixing bowl, combine the zucchini noodles, carrots, red cabbage, mushrooms, asparagus and grated ginger. Toss well and add the sesame oil, tamari and lime juice. Taste and adjust the seasoning with salt and pepper, if desired. Divide between 2 bowls or plates and garnish with the sesame seeds and scallions. Serve with chopsticks.

> note Spiral slicers, also called "spiralizers," are tools that make it supereasy to create noodles with a wide variety of vegetables. If you don't have a spiral slicer, you can easily make noodles with a vegetable peeler by running the peeler lengthwise down the zucchini for more of a linguine-style noodle.

Thai Almond Noodles

If you love Thai food as much as I do, you'll want to try this dish. I love the sweet and spicy flavors of peanut sauce, but here I've used almond butter as a healthy alternative to peanut butter. Zucchini noodles are a revelation if you are a noodle lover, but you can have a lot of fun playing with alternative vegetables to use for noodles. Try spiralizing sweet potatoes, carrots, cucumbers, summer squash, beets and even daikon radish.

Serves 2

Thai Almond Sauce

1½ tbsp (7 g) red pepper flakes

½ cup (118 ml) smooth almond butter

2 tbsp (30 ml) gluten-free tamari

¼ cup (60 ml) sesame oil

2 tbsp (30 ml) fresh lime juice

2 tbsp (30 ml) water

2 tbsp (30 ml) pure maple syrup

Salt

Thai Noodles

4 cups (427 g) zucchini noodles (from about 2 zucchini; see Notes) or 1 (12-oz [340-g]) package kelp noodles

2 cups (107 g) shredded red cabbage

1 cup (75 g) carrot noodles (from about 2 carrots; see Notes)

½ cup (78 g) edamame (frozen is okay)

¼ cup (31 g) seeded and slivered red or orange bell pepper

Salt

¼ cup (10 g) fresh cilantro, chopped, for garnish

¼ cup (10 g) fresh basil, chopped, for garnish

½ cup (70 g) dry-roasted cashews, for garnish

1 lime, cut into wedges, for garnish

For the Thai almond sauce, in a blender, combine all the sauce ingredients and puree until well incorporated. Set aside until ready to use. This will keep refrigerated for up to 1 week. Note: This sauce can taste quite strong when tried alone, but when it's used to dress the noodles, the taste mellows.

In a bowl, combine the zucchini noodles, red cabbage, carrot noodles, edamame and bell pepper and toss well. Add the sauce and toss again until the noodles are well coated. Adjust the seasoning with salt to taste. Portion the dressed noodles into 2 bowls and garnish with the cilantro, basil, cashews and lime. Serve immediately.

notes: This dish is best when the sauce is put on no more than 15 minutes before serving, as it tends to get watery the longer it sits. You can, however, make the noodle mix and the sauce separately, so all you have to do is toss and serve!

Have you ever made noodles from vegetables? If not, you're in for a real treat. You will need a tool called a spiral slicer to make them. They are available everywhere these days and are quite affordable. I have a small, handheld one that does a great job. You can also use a vegetable peeler to make wide flat noodles if you don't want to get a spiral slicer.

Kelp noodles are available in Asian supermarkets. They are a healthy raw vegan noodle alternative, made entirely from kelp. They are flavorless and a little crunchy but get softer after marinating in the sauce.

Teriyaki Kebabs

Very simple and affordable, this recipe is quick to throw together and can be modified with the vegetables you have on hand. Even though the dehydration time means you need to plan a little ahead, the preparation time is quite short. The short dehydration time in this recipe gives the vegetables a slightly cooked feeling, while still remaining raw. This is a great dish to bring to parties as a fancy appetizer!

Serves 2

Marinade
¼ cup (60 ml) pure maple syrup

¼ cup (60 ml) gluten-free tamari or soy sauce

1 tsp fresh lime juice

1½ tsp (8 ml) toasted sesame oil

¼ tsp garlic powder

1½ tsp (6 g) grated fresh ginger

¼ tsp red pepper flakes

Kebabs
1 tomato, cut into cubes

1 cup (165 g) chopped pineapple, cut into 1" (2.5-cm) chunks

1 medium zucchini, cut into cubes

½ cup (80 g) chopped red onion, cut into large chunks

½ cup (38 g) stemmed and halved shiitake mushrooms

For the marinade, in a bowl, combine all the marinade ingredients. Whisk well until everything is well mixed.

Toss all the vegetables in the marinade and allow to sit for 10 minutes. Remove the vegetables from the marinade and spread onto a solid dehydrator sheet. Dehydrate at 115°F (46°C) for 2 to 3 hours. The vegetables should be tender and feel slightly soft.

Assemble kebabs by skewering the vegetables along 8 wooden skewers. Serve with a side of the marinade for dipping.

> note Try the vegetables over cauliflower rice or tossed with greens as a "roasted vegetable" salad with avocado and toasted sesame seeds!

Bibimbop — Korean Cauliflower Rice Bowl

When transitioning to a high raw, plant-based diet, one of the most challenging cravings I struggled with was for refined carbohydrates, such as bread, pasta and white rice. Truly, having three or four dishes that satisfy this craving can be a lifesaver! I recommend having a favorite rice, pasta and bread or cracker substitute that you can make easily and often.

This "rice" bowl is one of my favorites. The combination of spicy fermented kimchi, fresh vegetables and meaty, marinated mushrooms is complex and healthy. And did I mention spicy? Don't worry, you can cut down the heat by skipping the gochujang if you'd like. This recipe may look long, but it actually is very quick to put together.

Serves 2 to 4 (depending on serving size)

Cauliflower Rice

4 cups (400 g) stemmed and roughly chopped cauliflower (about ½ large cauliflower)

1 cup (125 g) cashew pieces or whole cashews

2 tsp (10 g) salt, or to taste

4 tbsp (40 g) white sesame seeds

Gochujang Sauce

⅓ cup (80 g) miso

¼ cup (60 ml) pure maple syrup

⅓ cup (19 g) Korean chile flakes (see Note)

¼ cup (60 ml) gluten-free tamari

4 tsp (12 g) chopped garlic (about 4 cloves)

Bulgogi Marinated Mushrooms

1 tbsp (15 ml) gluten-free tamari

1 tbsp (15 ml) pure maple syrup

1½ tsp (8 ml) fresh lemon juice

1 tsp gochujang sauce

1 tsp finely minced garlic

1½ cups (100 g) shiitake mushrooms, sliced

For the cauliflower rice, in a food processor, pulse the cauliflower until the florets are broken up into rice-size pieces. Transfer to a large mixing bowl. Place the cashews in the food processor and pulse until broken up into small, crumbly pieces. Mix well with the cauliflower and season with salt. Mix in the sesame seeds. Set aside until ready to use.

For the gochujang sauce, in a blender, combine the miso, maple syrup, chile flakes, tamari and garlic and blend until smooth. Keep refrigerated until ready to use. This will keep in the refrigerator for up to 2 weeks.

For the bulgogi marinated mushrooms, in a mixing bowl, whisk together the tamari, maple syrup, lemon juice, 1 teaspoon of the gochujang sauce and the garlic. Add the sliced mushrooms and toss in the dressing to coat all the mushrooms well. Allow to marinate for a minimum of 10 to 15 minutes. Set aside until ready to use.

(continued)

Bibimbop—Korean Cauliflower Rice Bowl (continued)

Sesame Kale

2 cups (133 g) baby kale

1 tsp sesame oil

1 tsp sesame seeds

Pinch of sea salt

Bibimbop Bowls

½ cup (20 g) sprouts (I recommend sunflower sprouts)

1 medium cucumber, cut into matchsticks

1 medium carrot, peeled and cut into matchsticks

¼ cup (75 g) store-bought kimchi

1 tbsp (10 g) sesame seeds, for garnish

2 to 4 large scallions, sliced in ¼" (6-mm)-thick slices, for garnish

For the sesame kale, place the baby kale in a mixing bowl and add the sesame oil, sesame seeds and salt. Gently massage the greens until they are thoroughly coated with the oil and have begun to wilt. Set aside until ready to use.

To build the bowls, evenly divide the cauliflower rice between 2 large bowls. Working in a circle, place the sesame kale, sprouts, cucumber, carrot and kimchi on top of the rice in each bowl. In the center, place the bulgogi marinated mushrooms. Garnish with the sesame seeds and scallions, with the sauce on the side. When serving, I recommend mixing in the remaining gochujang sauce to taste, but serve the sauce on the side so you can control how spicy it is. Remember that you can always add more to taste, but you can't take it out once you've mixed it in. Other garnishes I recommend with this dish are various seaweeds, such as sushi nori, and other fresh vegetables, such as sliced radish, avocado and even Asian pear.

note   Korean chile flakes are moderately spiced with a fruity, flavorful undertone. They're quite delicious, but sometimes hard to find if you don't live in an area with a Korean or other international market.

You can replace them with several other easier-to-acquire peppers, however. Some suitable replacements are:

- cayenne pepper (this is much hotter, so start with less and add more as desired)
- crushed red pepper flakes (like the kind from your local pizza parlor)
- powdered chile de árbol, pasilla or New Mexico chile (found in most grocery stores in the Latin section or in Latin markets)
- paprika (a milder option)
- smoked paprika
- ground red pepper powder

Corn Tostadas

with **Mexican Slaw and Sunflower Frijoles**

High-protein sunflower seeds and flax will give you energy and fill you up but won't make you feel stuffed. You will still feel light and able to take on the day. Add more greens and try it as a taco salad as well! Or tear up the tortillas and use them for dip.

Serves 2 (2 tostadas per serving)

Tostada Shells

1⅛ cups (148 g) brown or gold flaxseeds

4½ cups (743 g) corn kernels

1¼ cups (296 ml) water

1½ tbsp (22 ml) fresh lime juice

2¼ tsp (18 g) chipotle powder

1 tsp ground cumin

1 tsp salt

Freshly ground black pepper

Sunflower Frijoles

½ cup (64 g) sunflower seeds

⅓ cup (73 ml) water, plus more as desired

¾ tbsp (11 ml) olive oil

¼ tsp garlic powder

¼ tsp chili powder

¼ tsp smoked paprika

½ tsp ground cumin

½ tsp salt, or more to taste

Freshly ground black pepper, if needed

For the tostada shells, in a dry blender or spice grinder, grind the flaxseeds into a fine powder. Transfer to a mixing bowl. Put the corn kernels into a blender along with the water, lime juice, chipotle powder, cumin, salt and pepper. Blend into a smooth slurry. Add this mixture to the ground flaxseeds and whisk together into a batter. On some solid nonstick dehydrator sheets, spread the tostada shell batter into 6 thin, flat, pancake-like shapes, and dehydrate for 2 hours on one side at 115°F (46°C).

After 2 hours, carefully flip and dehydrate for another 3 to 4 hours on mesh dehydrator screens, or until completely dry. If you don't have a dehydrator, you can use your oven to dry them out. Just spread them out on a baking sheet or cookie sheet lined with parchment paper and set the oven to its lowest setting, about 200°F (93°C). They will probably dry more quickly in the oven than the dehydrator, so check them every hour!

For the frijoles, soak the sunflower seeds for at least 1 hour in filtered water. When they are soaked, drain the seeds and rinse well with fresh water. Transfer the sunflower seeds to a food processor and process, adding the water little by little, until the sunflower seeds resemble refried beans. Add the olive oil, garlic powder, chili powder, smoked paprika, cumin and salt. Process a little longer to make sure everything is thoroughly mixed. Add more water if you would like a little thinner texture, as sunflower seeds tend to thicken up after a little time. Adjust the seasoning with salt and pepper to taste. Remove from the food processor and store in an airtight container in your refrigerator for up to 5 days. You can also make this in your blender.

(continued)

Corn Tostadas with Mexican Slaw and Sunflower Frijoles (continued)

Mexican Slaw

1 cup (54 g) shredded green cabbage

¼ cup (13 g) shredded red cabbage

⅛ cup (5 g) fresh cilantro, chopped

½ carrot, shredded

½ jalapeño pepper, seeded and sliced (optional)

1 radish, sliced

1½ tsp (7 ml) fresh lime juice

1 tsp agave nectar

⅛ tsp salt

To Assemble

1 avocado, pitted, peeled and sliced

½ cup (118 ml) Chipotle Salsa (page 70) or store-bought

¼ cup (10 g) cilantro

For the Mexican slaw, in a mixing bowl, combine the green and red cabbage, cilantro, carrot, jalapeño (if using) and radish. Mix well and then add the lime juice, agave and salt. Toss well until everything is thoroughly coated. Set aside until ready to use. This will keep refrigerated for several days.

To assemble the tostadas, take 1 finished tostada shell and spread one-quarter of the frijoles onto the shell. Place one-quarter of the sliced avocado on top of the frijoles and top with one-quarter of the slaw. Garnish with a little salsa and cilantro. Repeat to form 3 more tostadas.

> note The tostadas make a great option for dipping raw vegan corn chips! They're super-healthy and really hold up to salsa and guacamole.

Almond and Sun-Dried Tomato Hummus Wrap

Wraps are a great item to take with you when you're on the go. You may be surprised to think of having collard greens raw, but they substitute admirably for a wheat wrap. It's a nice change from daily salads, but just as nutritious. Just be sure to trim the stem down the center of the leaf to help it fold up nicely.

Serves 2 (2 wraps per serving)

Sun-Dried Tomato and Almond Hummus

½ cup (78 g) raw almonds, soaked in water overnight

2 tbsp (30 ml) tahini

2 tbsp (30 ml) olive oil

2 tbsp (2 g) sun-dried tomatoes, soaked for 20 minutes in ½ cup (120 ml) water

¼ cup (60 ml) water, plus more as needed

1 clove garlic

½ tsp sea salt, plus more to taste

1 tbsp (15 ml) fresh lemon juice, plus more to taste, if desired

Pinch of cayenne pepper (optional)

Lemon Tahini Sauce

3 tbsp (45 ml) fresh orange juice

1 tbsp (15 ml) fresh lemon juice

2 tbsp (30 ml) tahini

1 tbsp (15 ml) cider vinegar

1½ tsp (8 ml) Dijon mustard

1 small clove garlic

½ tsp sea salt

Freshly ground black pepper

3 tbsp (45 ml) water, as needed

Collard Wraps

4 large collard leaves, stems removed and trimmed down the length of the leaf

½ cup (186 g) sliced medium cherry tomatoes

1 organic cucumber, washed and sliced into half-moons

½ cup (90 g) seeded and julienned red bell pepper

½ cup (62 g) matchstick-cut carrot

½ cup (27 g) shredded red or green cabbage

1 avocado, pitted, peeled and sliced

¼ cup (10 g) fresh cilantro, stemmed

⅛ cup (2 g) alfalfa, radish or broccoli sprouts

For the hummus, drain and rinse the almonds and discard the soak water. Place the almonds in a food processor along with the tahini, olive oil, sun-dried tomatoes, water, garlic, salt, lemon juice and cayenne. Puree until smooth and then adjust the seasoning with more salt or more lemon juice, as desired. If you need to thin the mixture to help it become smooth in the processor, add water as needed until it purees more easily. Keep refrigerated in an airtight container for up to a week.

For the lemon tahini sauce, hand whisk all the sauce ingredients well in a bowl or mix in a blender. Set aside until ready to use. This will keep refrigerated for up to a week.

For each wrap, lay 1 large collard leaf on a cutting board, like a burrito wrap. In the middle of the wrap, spread about 2 tablespoons (30 ml) of the hummus down the center of the leaf, and then place a few slices of tomato, sliced cucumber, some bell pepper, carrot, cabbage, avocado slices, a few sprigs of cilantro, and a small handful of sprouts. Drizzle about 2 tablespoons (30 ml) of lemon tahini sauce inside to finish and roll up into a burrito. Finish building the rest of the wraps and serve with some of the lemon tahini sauce on the side.

Meze Platter

with Spicy Beet Salad, Fig Pâté, Flax Crackers and Cucumber Raita

With so many flavors and textures, this Mediterranean-inspired platter goes over big for a casual gathering, dinner party or special event. One of my favorite things about a plant-based diet is the greater variety that you can experience. For this platter, feel free to change the ingredients you use. Substitute some sliced fresh fruit, some pickles or your favorite nuts. The idea is to have a nice mix: a little spicy, a little sweet, a little creamy and with a hint of crunchy.

Makes 8 to 10 servings

Beet Salad

1 beet

1 apple

¼ cup (32 g) dried apricots, chopped

¼ cup (32 g) golden raisins

¼ cup (25 g) chopped green onion

2 tbsp (8 g) chopped fresh flat-leaf parsley

¼ cup (33 g) pitted and chopped black sun-dried olives

1 tsp minced garlic

1 tbsp (15 ml) fresh lemon juice

2 tbsp (30 ml) pure maple syrup

2 tbsp (30 ml) harissa (see Note)

½ tsp salt

¼ cup (60 ml) olive oil

Fig Pâté

1 cup (149 g) dried Mission figs

1½ tsp (1 g) ground coriander

2 tbsp (30 ml) agave nectar

Meze Platter

½ cup (118 ml) Cucumber Raita (page 105)

¼ cup (62 g) Cashew Ricotta (page 61)

½ cup (50 g) olives

12 to 16 Tostada Shells (page 47), broken into chips, or crackers of your choice

For the beet salad, wash and peel the beet. Slice it very, very thinly, using a knife, a food processor or a mandoline slicer. The more thinly you slice the beet, the better for this recipe! Wash, core and slice the apple as well and place in a mixing bowl along with the beet. Add the chopped apricots, raisins, green onion, parsley and olives. Mix well. In a separate bowl, whisk together the garlic, lemon juice, maple syrup, harissa, salt and olive oil. Mix in the dressing with the beet salad and toss well. Allow to marinate for at least 1 hour before serving. Keep refrigerated for up to 1 week. This salad gets better with time, as the beets become softer and the flavor more complex!

For the fig pâté, soak the figs for 1 hour, then drain and discard the soak water. Cut off the stems. Place the soaked figs in a food processor and add the ground coriander and agave. Process until smooth.

To serve, create a platter featuring separate arrangements of the beet salad, fig pâté, cucumber raita, cashew ricotta and olives. Serve with crackers of your choice or with a raw flax cracker, such as the tostada shells.

note Harissa is a Middle Eastern chili paste with hints of garlic and cumin. You can buy it at most grocery stores or specialty shops. I like to get mine at my local Trader Joe's.

Sweet Red Thai Coconut Curry

with Zucchini Noodles, Pineapple, Tomato, Sprouts and Cashews

A healthy and brightly flavored dish, with hints of herbs, lemongrass and chile. So full of flavor and great with almost any vegetables you have on hand, but you must try it with the pineapple. The sweet and savory flavor combination is such a surprise. You will definitely want to have an extra zucchini on hand, because you will be coming back for seconds.

Serves 2

Thai Curry Sauce
½ (3.5-oz [104-ml]) can coconut milk

1½ tsp (8 ml) gluten-free tamari

1½ tbsp (23 ml) red curry paste

1 tbsp (15 ml) agave nectar

1½ tsp (8 ml) olive oil

1½ tsp (3 g) curry powder

¾ tsp peeled and grated fresh ginger

¾ tbsp (7 g) chopped red onion

¼ cup (35 g) raw cashews

¾ tsp sea salt

Thai Curry Bowl
2 zucchini

1 jalapeño pepper, seeded and very thinly sliced (optional)

1 cup (154 g) chopped pineapple (frozen is okay)

1 tomato, cut into wedges

¼ cup (37 g) bell pepper, seeded and thinly sliced

1 cup (40 g) spicy sprouts, such as radish or daikon, for garnish

¼ cup (27 g) cashews, roughly chopped, for garnish

¼ cup (8 g) fresh basil, chopped, for garnish

¼ cup (8 g) fresh mint, chopped, for garnish

Salt, to taste

2 lime wedges, for serving

For the Thai curry sauce, in a blender, combine all the sauce ingredients. Blend for about 2 minutes, until smooth.

To build the Thai curry bowl, peel the zucchini and use a spiral slicer or peeler to cut them lengthwise into ribbons. Place in a mixing bowl along with the jalapeño (if using), pineapple, tomato and bell pepper. Toss well. Add about 1 cup (236 ml) of the curry sauce right before serving and mix well. Divide between 2 bowls and garnish with spicy sprouts, chopped cashews, basil and mint. Adjust the seasoning with salt to taste, if desired. Serve with the lime wedges.

note It's best to keep the vegetables and sauce separate until right before ready to serve, as the sauce tends to get watery and separate.

Summer Vegetable Chili

Some dishes really hit the spot when you are craving something hearty, and this raw chili is one of them! Feel free to change up the vegetables of this chunky raw stew, for variety. I like to serve this mildly warm or at least at room temperature. You might want to leave your vegetables out for one hour to come to room temperature if you're making it right before serving. You can also warm it gently in a saucepan over very low heat until it's just warm, but not cooked.

Makes 1 quart (946 ml); serves 4

Chili Vegetables
2 small zucchini, chopped

2 medium carrots, peeled and chopped

1 cup (100 g) walnuts

1 cup (71 g) button mushrooms

1 cup (150 g) fresh corn kernels

2 tbsp (22 g) chopped red onion

Chili Base
4 large tomatoes, cut into quarters and seeded

1 tbsp (5 g) sun-dried tomato

2 tbsp (18 g) raisins

2 cloves garlic

1 jalapeño pepper (optional)

1 tbsp (15 ml) olive oil

1 tsp chili powder

1 tsp paprika

1 tsp ground cumin

1 tsp ground coriander

1 tsp salt, or more to taste

2 pinches of chipotle powder or other chili powder

Toppings
1 avocado, pitted, peeled and sliced

¼ cup (14 g) green onion

For the chili vegetables, in a food processor fitted with the S-blade, combine the zucchini, carrots, walnuts and mushrooms and pulse, until chunky but not pureed. Transfer to a bowl and mix with the corn and red onion. Set aside.

For the chili base, in a blender, combine the tomatoes, sun-dried tomato, raisins, garlic, jalapeño (if using), olive oil, spices, salt and chipotle powder, then transfer to the chili vegetables. Stir well. Divide the finished chili among 4 bowls. Top with the avocado and green onion.

note   This recipe actually improves with time and will be good for up to a week as the flavors meld and mellow. It will separate as it sits, but don't worry! Just give it a stir, and you'll be good to go. The nature of this recipe is to become watery as it sits, because the salt will slowly draw out the moisture in the vegetables.

Walnut-Chorizo Tacos

with **Kiwi Salsa** and **Guacamole**

Have a taco night and try out a build-your-own taco bar with the recipes here—kids will love it, and so will you. There is something about Mexican food that translates especially well to raw vegan cuisine. Tacos are a perfect dish to try—and there's no dehydration or waiting for anything to set up, so it's easy to throw together at short notice.

Serves 4

Chorizo
¼ cup (30 g) walnuts

¼ cup (30 g) pecans

¼ cup (30 g) pumpkin seeds

1½ tbsp (23 ml) chili paste (optional)

⅛ tsp ground cloves

¼ tsp salt

¼ tsp freshly ground black pepper

2 tbsp (30 ml) olive oil

1 tsp chili powder

1 tsp fresh oregano

⅛ tsp cayenne pepper

⅛ tsp ground cumin

Raw Vegan Sour Cream
1 cup (137 g) cashews

½ cup (118 ml) water, or to taste

¼ cup (60 ml) fresh lemon juice, or more to taste

Pinch of salt

For the walnut chorizo, in a food processor, combine the walnuts, pecans and pumpkin seeds and pulse until they are crumbly but not powdery. Transfer the mixture to a mixing bowl and add the chili paste (if using), cloves, salt, pepper, olive oil, chili powder, oregano, cayenne and cumin. Mix well until the spices are evenly mixed and the nut mixture is coated. Set aside until ready to use. This will keep for up to a month refrigerated in an airtight container.

For the raw vegan sour cream, soak the cashews for a minimum of 2 hours or overnight in purified water, then drain and discard the soak water. Put the cashews in a blender and add the water, lemon juice and salt. Puree until smooth.

(continued)

Walnut-Chorizo Tacos with Kiwi Salsa and Guacamole (continued)

Kiwi Salsa

2 kiwis

1 medium mango

1 tbsp (15 ml) fresh lime juice

Pinch of salt, or more to taste

¼ cup (40 g) minced red onion

¼ cup (10 g) fresh cilantro, chopped

1 jalapeño pepper, seeded and minced

Guacamole

2 avocados, pitted and peeled

2 tbsp (30 ml) fresh lime juice

¼ cup (40 g) minced red onion

¼ tsp salt

¼ cup (10 g) fresh cilantro, chopped

Taco Shells

1 medium head green or red cabbage

For the kiwi salsa, peel and chop the kiwis into a fine dice. Peel, pit and chop the mango. Place the kiwi and mango in a mixing bowl along with the lime juice, salt, red onion, cilantro and jalapeño. Toss well until well combined. The salsa will keep for up to 2 days in the refrigerator.

For the guacamole, in a bowl, combine the avocados, lime juice, red onion, salt and cilantro and mash everything together. Serve immediately.

To assemble the tacos, carefully remove and discard the outer leaves of the cabbage. Then, start to carefully remove leaves to use as shells. I like to chop off the stem of the cabbage, as this helps the leaves separate from the cabbage without tearing. Expect to lose a few leaves in this process, as it can be tricky at first! Place some of the chorizo in the shell and top with the raw vegan sour cream, guacamole and kiwi salsa.

note   Most of the components in this dish can be made ahead of time and will keep very nicely; however, you will find that guacamole is one thing that does not keep well as it tends to brown. If you want to preserve your guacamole, try this trick: Place a layer of plastic wrap right on the surface of the guacamole and press down to seal the surface from the air. The less contact with air, the better your yummy guacamole will keep!

Raw Eggplant Manicotti

Creamy ricotta, fresh tangy tomato sauce and a drizzle of the best olive oil. What makes Italian food so wonderful is its simplicity and use of the best-quality ingredients. With this version of raw vegan manicotti, you won't miss the pasta. Sliced and marinated eggplant stands in for the pasta here. Being gluten-free has never been so delicious!

Makes 10 to 12 manicotti rolls; serves 4

Manicotti Shells
1 small globe eggplant (2 lb [907g])

Salt and freshly ground black pepper

Olive oil, for brushing the eggplant

Cashew Ricotta
1½ cups (255 g) cashews

¼ cup (60 ml) water, plus more as needed

1 tbsp (8 g) nutritional yeast

1 tsp sea salt

Freshly ground black pepper

¼ cup (12 g) chopped fresh chives

Marinated Vegetable Filling
2 cups (144 g) quartered cremini mushrooms

¼ cup (60 ml) olive oil, divided

Salt and freshly ground black pepper

2 cups (50 g) arugula

For the shells, slice the eggplant lengthwise into ⅛-inch (3-mm)-thick strips. Lay the eggplant slices on a baking sheet with some paper towels underneath them and sprinkle with salt and pepper. Brush lightly with olive oil. Allow to sit for 30 minutes before using or dehydrate for 1 hour at 118°F (48°C) to soften them more completely, then gently dab with a paper towel to remove excess moisture.

For the cashew ricotta, soak the nuts in water overnight, then rinse well. Place the cashews in a food processor and pulse until fairly smooth. Add water as needed to help the nuts process. Add the nutritional yeast, salt and pepper and pulse again. Fold in the chives by hand. Note that if you add them to the food processor, your cheese will taste fine but will turn green. It's prettier folded in by hand.

For the vegetable filling, toss the mushrooms with 2 tablespoons (30 ml) of the olive oil and season with salt and pepper to taste. Place in a dehydrator and dehydrate at 118°F (48°C) for 1 to 2 hours, or until they look roasted. When they are finished dehydrating, transfer to a bowl and toss with the arugula, remaining 2 tablespoons (30 ml) of oil, and salt and pepper to taste. Set aside for 30 minutes at room temperature until you're ready to assemble the manicotti.

For the manicotti rolls, after blotting the eggplant slices to remove any excess liquid, place 1 tablespoon (15 ml) of the cashew ricotta in the center of each strip. Top with a small handful of the vegetable filling. Roll each manicotti and allow to rest on a plate or tray lined with deli paper or a paper towel until ready to serve. The rolls can be stored like this for several days, if you change the paper underneath them, although the eggplant will darken slightly. I don't recommend trying to freeze these.

(continued)

Raw Eggplant Manicotti (continued)

Heirloom Tomato Sauce

1 very ripe heirloom tomato or the softest vine-ripened tomato you can find

2 tbsp (30 ml) olive oil

¼ cup (12 g) minced fresh chives

1 clove garlic, minced

1 tsp sea salt

Freshly ground black pepper

To Serve

¼ cup (12 g) chopped fresh chives, plus some left whole

1 tbsp (8 g) nutritional yeast

16 cherry tomatoes, halved

For the heirloom tomato sauce, chop the tomato very finely by hand until it is almost liquefied. You can do this in the food processor or blender, but it will not have as beautiful a texture as doing it by hand. If you can't get heirloom tomatoes, a blender or food processor will do a better job on hothouse tomatoes. Stir in the olive oil, chives, garlic, salt and pepper to taste.

To serve, spoon some of the heirloom tomato sauce onto each of 4 plates. Arrange 3 of the manicotti on each serving of the sauce and garnish with some chopped and whole chives and some nutritional yeast. Finish with a few cherry tomato halves on the plate. Serve immediately and enjoy!

> note You can make the shells ahead of time and keep them in a covered dish in your refrigerator. Just add the sauce before serving, and you're ready to go! I also like to let them sit at room temperature for about 30 minutes before serving, so they soften up a little.

Pumpkin Seed and Cilantro Pesto Pizza

Pizza, pizza! If you're trying to eat a healthy diet, you don't have to give up pizza if you make it raw. There are infinite varieties you can dream up—this is just one of my favorites. You could think of these also as flatbreads or bruschetta. I think you will enjoy having these on hand to snack on or to take to a party!

Serves 2 to 4

The Basics

Raw Vegan Pizza Crust

1½ cups (210 g) sunflower seeds, soaked in water for 2 hours, then drained and rinsed

1½ cups (275 g) thinly sliced zucchini rounds

1 small tomato

¾ cup (84 g) ground flaxseeds

2 tbsp (30 ml) olive oil

2 tbsp (6 g) chopped fresh basil

2 tbsp (3 g) chopped fresh rosemary

1 tbsp (4 g) chopped fresh oregano

2 tsp (10 g) salt

Cashew Cheese

1 cup (113 g) cashews, soaked in water for 2 hours, then drained and rinsed

1 tbsp (15 ml) fresh lemon juice

Water, as needed

1 tbsp (8 g) nutritional yeast

1 tbsp (2 g) chopped fresh rosemary

1 tbsp (3 g) chopped fresh chives

1 tbsp (3 g) chopped fresh basil

1 tsp salt

Cilantro Pesto Sauce

1 cup (40 g) fresh cilantro

½ cup (71 g) pumpkin seeds

¼ cup (60 ml) olive oil

1 clove garlic, chopped

Pinch of salt

Per Pesto Pizza

1 fresh tomato, thinly sliced

½ zucchini, thinly sliced lengthwise

2 radishes, thinly sliced

⅛ cup (17 g) black olives, pitted and sliced

1 tbsp (3 g) chopped fresh basil

First, let's make the basics. For the pizza crust, in a food processor, combine the sunflower seeds, zucchini and tomato. Puree until fairly smooth (at least no large chunks) and transfer the mixture to a large mixing bowl. Add the ground flax, olive oil, basil, rosemary, oregano and salt. Mix well. On a nonstick Teflex dehydrator sheet, spread the mixture to 4 circles each ¼ inch (6 mm) thick and 6 to 8 inches (15 to 20 cm) in diameter. Dehydrate at 110°F (43°C) for 5 hours. Flip the crusts and remove the nonstick sheets. Dehydrate for another hour on mesh dehydrator sheets. Store in an airtight container or resealable plastic bag in your refrigerator until ready to use.

For the cashew cheese, in a food processor, combine the cashews and lemon juice and process until smooth, adding a little water as necessary to help the cheese become creamy. Transfer the mixture to a large mixing bowl. Add the nutritional yeast, rosemary, chives, basil and salt. Stir until everything is well incorporated. Keep the mixture refrigerated until ready to use.

For the pesto sauce, in a food processor, combine the cilantro, pumpkin seeds, olive oil, garlic and salt. Puree until fairly smooth. Store in an airtight container in your refrigerator until ready to use.

Now let's make pizza! For each pesto pizza, spread one-quarter of the pesto onto a pizza base. Top with thin slices of tomato. Arrange the sliced zucchini and radishes on the pesto. Top with 2 tablespoons (56 g) of the cashew cheese and the olives and chopped basil. Serve immediately.

Hawaiian Mushroom Pizza

with Pineapple and Sun-Dried Tomato Sauce

Let pizza be your canvas! Have a pizza party and mix up your toppings so your family and friends can build their own. This version of Hawaiian pizza has mushrooms instead of ham, which are complemented by the sweet pineapple. I love fruit with savory dishes, especially on pizza. The tart, juicy flavor really pops with the mildly salty and spicy notes.

Serves 1

Sun-Dried Tomato Sauce
¼ cup (24 g) sun-dried tomato, in oil

½ cup (65 g) seeded and chopped red bell pepper

1 tbsp (15 ml) olive oil

¼ tsp garlic powder

¼ tsp red pepper flakes

½ tsp sea salt

Marinated Mushrooms
½ cup (26 g) mushrooms, sliced (see Note)

1 tbsp (15 ml) olive oil

⅛ tsp sea salt

Per Hawaiian Pizza
1 Raw Vegan Pizza Crust (page 65)

¼ cup (113 g) Cashew Cheese (page 65)

⅛ cup (40 g) chopped fresh pineapple (frozen is okay)

½ tsp red pepper flakes (optional)

To make the tomato sauce, in a blender, combine the sun-dried tomato, bell pepper, olive oil, garlic powder, red pepper flakes and salt and puree until smooth.

For the marinated mushrooms, in a bowl, toss the sliced mushrooms with the olive oil and sea salt. Allow to marinate for at least 30 minutes.

To assemble the pizza, spread each pizza crust with ¼ cup (60 ml) of the tomato sauce. Top with dollops of the cashew cheese, half of the marinated mushrooms, the pineapple and the red pepper flakes, if desired. Serve immediately.

> note: You can use cooked mushrooms. Some people prefer not to consume raw mushrooms, and it's perfectly fine to cook them lightly for this recipe.

Spaghetti and "Meatballs"

Kids love pasta, and if you don't tell them it's raw vegan, they probably won't know the difference! This is a versatile basic sauce and pasta recipe—mix it up with different vegetables, if you'd like. I highly recommend eating the meatballs directly out of the dehydrator, spiralizing the zucchini when it's room temperature and very gently warming the sauce in a pan over low heat. This dish is as close to comfort food as you'll get, so it's better not served cold straight out of the refrigerator.

Serves 2

Spaghetti Sauce

2 medium tomatoes

1 tbsp (6 g) sun-dried tomatoes, soaked in water for 20 minutes, then chopped

1 date

¼ red bell pepper, seeded and chopped

2 tbsp (30 ml) olive oil

½ tsp sea salt or Himalayan pink salt, plus more to taste

¼ tsp dried oregano

½ tsp crushed red pepper flakes, or to taste

½ tsp garlic powder

1 tsp cider vinegar

⅛ cup (15 g) walnuts

Zucchini Pasta

4 large zucchini

¼ cup (15 g) chopped fresh flat-leaf parsley, plus more for garnish

Red pepper flakes, for garnish

"Meatballs"

1 cup (114 g) walnuts

1 cup (65 g) mushrooms

1 tbsp (6 g) sun-dried tomato

1 tbsp (3 g) fresh basil

1 tbsp (15 g) minced red onion

¼ tsp ground cumin

¼ tsp fresh rosemary, finely chopped, plus more for garnish

¼ tsp salt

1 tsp fresh oregano, finely chopped, plus more for garnish

For the sauce, in a blender, combine all the sauce ingredients and pulse until you have achieved a chunky tomato sauce texture. You can also do this step in a food processor.

For the pasta, using a spiral slicer, slice the zucchini into pasta ribbons, or use a vegetable peeler to make long, flat noodles down the length of the zucchini. Toss with the parsley, and as much sauce as you would like—probably about ½ cup (120 ml) of sauce per serving. Garnish with more chopped parsley, and with additional red pepper flakes if you like it spicy.

For the meatballs, in a food processor or blender, combine the walnuts, mushrooms and sun-dried tomato and process until chunky. Transfer to a bowl and mix in the basil, red onion, cumin, rosemary, salt and oregano until well incorporated. Form into balls about 1 inch (2.5 cm) in diameter. Place them in a food dehydrator and dehydrate for 1 hour at 115°F (46°C).

To serve, divide the zucchini noodles between 2 bowls or plates and top with more sauce, meatballs and additional fresh herbs to taste.

notes: If you are making this for kids, you might want to skip the red pepper flakes in the sauce recipe, so it's as mild as possible.

Also, if you don't have a dehydrator, you can dry the meatballs in your oven on its lowest setting, on a nonstick baking sheet. Just make sure you check them every 30 minutes, as they will dry faster in the oven than in a dehydrator.

Fresh Corn and Mushroom Tamales

with Chipotle Salsa

Tamales make a beautiful presentation served in the corn husk. You can use either fresh or dried, but if you choose dried you might want to soak them for at least 30 minutes to be able to work with them. Also, if you have never eaten fresh, raw corn, you are in for a treat: I also like it on the cob with a little olive oil and sea salt, almost like street corn.

Serves 4 to 6

12 corn husks, fresh or dried

Fresh Corn Masa

3 cups (450 g) fresh corn kernels (from about 4 ears)

½ cup (68 g) cashews or macadamias, soaked in water for 1 hour, then drained and rinsed

1 tbsp (7 g) onion powder

1 tsp salt

3 tbsp (45 ml) fresh lemon juice

Pinch of freshly ground black pepper

1¼ cups (130 g) oat flour (made from ground rolled oats)

2 tbsp (8 g) psyllium powder

Tamale Filling

¾ cup (54 g) finely diced portobello mushroom

3 tbsp (30 g) finely minced red onion

2 tbsp (14 g) Mexican chili powder

2 tsp (16 g) nutritional yeast

2 tsp (10 ml) fresh lemon juice

½ tsp salt

½ tsp minced garlic

Chipotle Salsa

2 cups (356 g) halved fresh heirloom cherry tomatoes

½ cup (55 g) chopped white onion

2 small cloves garlic, chopped

½ jalapeño pepper, chopped

2 chipotle peppers in adobo, plus 1 tsp of the adobo sauce

1 tsp kosher salt

½ tsp freshly ground black pepper

½ cup (20 g) fresh cilantro

Juice of 1 lime

If using dried corn husks, soak the husks in warm water and set aside to soften for 30 minutes to an hour while you build the tamales.

For the fresh corn masa, in a food processor, combine the corn and cashews with the onion powder, salt, lemon juice and pepper and process until smooth. Transfer to a medium mixing bowl. Add the oat flour and psyllium powder and stir to combine well. Using a ½-cup (120-ml) measure to portion your masa, create small oblong corn masa cakes, about ¼ inch (5 mm) thick, on a nonstick dehydrator sheet. Dehydrate in a dehydrator set at 135°F (57°C) for 1 hour. Turn the cakes over, lower the temperature to 115°F (46°C) and continue to dehydrate for another 30 minutes.

For the filling, in a bowl, combine all the filling ingredients and mix well. Allow to marinate for about 30 minutes at room temperature before using to build the tamales.

For the chipotle salsa, in a food processor or high-powered blender, combine all ingredients and pulse until everything is evenly blended. Taste and adjust the salt and pepper as needed. Add more chipotle peppers if you like it extra spicy. Remove from the food processor or blender and refrigerate.

To assemble the tamales, remove the corn masa cakes from the dehydrator and create a small indentation in the center of each with your finger. Place 1½ tablespoons (23 ml) of the filling into the indentation and gently fold the corn cake from each side to almost cover the filling. Place the tamales back in the dehydrator, set at 115°F (46°C), for 30 minutes. To serve the tamales, place them in the center of a corn husk. Serve the tamales warm, with chipotle salsa over the top.

Some Like It Hot

Nourishing Lightly Cooked Vegan Entrées

I began my career as chef of a raw vegan restaurant called Cru in Los Angeles in 2006. When we first opened, we were 100 percent raw. After about a year, I added some cooked food to our menu during the winter to give people something warm to eat during the colder months. It was very important to me to present the healthiest, most nutrient-dense and easy-to-digest cooked dishes, as this was our mission as a raw vegan restaurant. I was a little taken aback by how popular our cooked dishes were almost immediately, because weren't we a raw vegan restaurant, after all?

Later, I came to appreciate that our customers liked the healthy, gluten-free way we were cooking, and I'm sure they liked the way it made them feel. I hope you do, too! A few of the recipes are versions of ones I served to my customers at Cru, such as the Gluten-Free Mac and Cheese (page 86) and the Freekeh Risotto with Roasted Trumpet Mushrooms (page 85). Others are favorites of mine that I have created over the years in different vegan restaurants. All of them share the philosophy of letting the vegetables shine as the star of the show.

Mushroom Scallops

with Nasturtium Kombu Pesto

Serves 4

Nasturtium Kombu Pesto

0.5 oz (14 g) kombu (see Notes)

2 cups (473 ml) water

1 cup (125 g) walnuts

1 or 2 cloves garlic

4 cups (80 g) baby arugula

1 cup (20 g) nasturtium leaves (optional)

1 tsp sea salt

1 tbsp (8 g) nutritional yeast

Zest and juice (30 ml) of 1 lemon

¾ cup (177 ml) olive oil

Mushroom Scallops

8 large king oyster mushrooms (see Notes)

2 tbsp (30 ml) melted coconut oil

Salt and freshly ground black pepper

Garnishes

1 cup (20 g) nasturtium leaves and flowers

1 lemon, cut into wedges

This recipe is from a dinner I catered celebrating edible flowers. Nasturtiums are a delicious and common edible flower.

Mushrooms look so convincing as scallops that you might fool your friends. They are tender and juicy, and they sear beautifully. Try to get the largest king oyster mushrooms possible for the most convincing scallops. Be very careful when forming the scallops as mushrooms can be fragile.

For the pesto, soak the kombu in the water for 15 minutes. You should have one 3 x 7-inch (7.5 x 18-cm) sheet. After it's been soaked, remove the kombu from the water and set the water aside in case you need to thin your pesto. Cut the kombu into rough pieces about 1 inch (2.5 cm) square and transfer to a food processor or blender. In a food processor, combine the kombu with the walnuts, garlic, arugula, nasturtium leaves (if using), salt, nutritional yeast, and lemon zest and juice. Pulse a few times to create a chunky mixture. Slowly add the olive oil, and process more until smooth. You will have chunks of kombu, but that's okay! Process for 2 to 3 minutes, or until smooth. Add kombu soak water if you like a thinner pesto.

For the mushroom scallops, cut the mushroom stems into 1-inch (2.5-cm)-long pieces. Save the tops to eat later or cut them into rounds as well. In a nonstick pan, heat the coconut oil over medium heat and add the mushroom pieces, cut side down. Cook for 2 to 3 minutes, or until browned. Turn the scallops to the other side and cook for another 2 to 3 minutes. Season liberally with salt and pepper. Remove from the heat and serve immediately.

To serve, spread some of the pesto on each plate. Arrange the scallops on the pesto and garnish with nasturtium leaves and lemon wedges.

notes: Kombu is an edible form of kelp sold in large, dried sheets. It's great for soups and stews.

What if you can't find king oyster mushrooms? Use jumbo portobello caps or large white cremini mushrooms, carefully cutting the caps into a scallop shape. I used a ring mold to get a perfect round shape.

Cauliflower Steak

with Chimichurri

Cauliflower steaks are a wonderful option for a dinner party and can be served with any number of sauces. I love this chimichurri for its bright, herbaceous punch. These steaks are oven-roasted, but they can also be cooked completely on your stovetop in a heavy-bottomed pan, if desired. Just be sure to test the center with a knife to make sure they are tender in the thickest part of the stem, which cooks the slowest.

Serves 4

Chimichurri

1 cup (60 g) firmly packed fresh flat-leaf parsley, trimmed of thick stems

2 tbsp (4 g) fresh oregano leaves, or 2 tsp (2 g) dried oregano

3 to 4 garlic cloves

⅓ cup (83 ml) olive oil

2 tbsp (30 ml) red wine vinegar

½ tsp sea salt

⅛ tsp freshly ground black pepper

¼ tsp red pepper flakes

Cauliflower Steaks

2 large heads cauliflower

3 to 4 tbsp (45 to 60 ml) olive oil, plus a few tbsp more for searing

Salt and freshly ground black pepper

1 lemon cut in wedges

For the chimichurri, in a food processor or blender, combine the parsley, oregano and garlic and roughly puree. Transfer to a small bowl. Stir in the olive oil, vinegar, salt and pepper and red pepper flakes. Adjust the seasonings. Serve immediately or refrigerate for up to 2 days. If chilled, return the chimichurri to room temperature before serving.

For the cauliflower steaks, preheat your oven to 350°F (180°C). Each head of cauliflower will give you only 2 steaks at the most, due to the delicate structure of the heads. In my experience, the best way to proceed is to cut both sides off, leaving a 2-inch (5-cm)-thick slab of cauliflower in the middle, and then carefully cut the slab in half to form your steaks. Coat the steaks with the olive oil, salt and pepper and roast, uncovered, in your oven for 15 to 20 minutes, turning once, until slightly golden and fork-tender. Remove from the oven and set aside until ready to use. Heat a few tablespoons of olive oil in a heavy-bottomed skillet. Sear the cauliflower steaks for a minute or two on each side before serving.

Serve the steaks dressed with the chimichurri and lemon wedges on top.

note: Cook the extra pieces of cauliflower along with the steak and serve on top, if you don't have any other use for them.

Portobello Steak

with Red Wine Sauce and Garlic Mashed Cauliflower

An elegant meal that is perfect for special occasions—try mixing up the vegetables for variety. It would be great with heirloom baby carrots in the summer or roasted radishes in the spring. If you are a lover of mashed potatoes (what, that's not a meal in itself?), you will want to make the mashed cauliflower often.

Serves 2

Garlic Mashed Cauliflower
1 small head cauliflower

½ tsp garlic powder

2 tbsp (30 ml) almond milk

1 tbsp (8 g) nutritional yeast

Salt and freshly ground black pepper, to taste

Red Wine Sauce
2 tbsp (30 ml) extra virgin olive oil

2 shallots, minced

3 cloves garlic, minced

½ tsp dried thyme

2 cups (473 ml) red wine

2 tbsp (30 ml) Dijon mustard

½ tsp potato starch, cornstarch or arrowroot powder

2 tbsp (28 g) cold vegan butter, such as Earth Balance brand

⅛ tsp ground white pepper

Salt

Portobello Steaks
4 large portobello caps

Olive oil

Salt and freshly ground black pepper

1 large bunch asparagus, ends trimmed

Olive oil

Salt and freshly ground black pepper

To make the mashed cauliflower, place a steamer in a saucepan and fill the pan with water to just below the bottom of the steamer. Bring the water to a boil. Add the cauliflower, cover and steam for 10 minutes. Remove from the steamer and transfer to a food processor. Pulse until the cauliflower is broken up. Add the garlic powder, almond milk and nutritional yeast and pulse until the cauliflower becomes creamy like mashed potatoes. Season to taste with salt and pepper.

For the red wine sauce, heat the olive oil in a skillet over low heat and sauté the shallots and garlic for 2 minutes. Add the thyme and sauté for 1 minute more. Whisk in the red wine and mustard. Bring to a simmer and reduce by two-thirds, about 30 minutes. Whisk in the potato starch and the cold vegan butter. Cook for 1 to 2 more minutes over low heat. Remove from the heat and transfer to a blender, then puree until smooth. Season to taste with white pepper and salt.

For the portobello steaks, preheat your oven to 350°F (180°C). Remove the stems of all the mushroom caps and carefully remove the gills on the underside of the caps, using the side of a spoon. Brush off any dirt and coat lightly with oil on both sides. Season liberally with salt and pepper. Place the portobello caps on an oiled baking sheet and roast for 15 to 20 minutes, or until tender and juicy.

To cook the asparagus, coat thoroughly with oil, salt and pepper. Place on a baking sheet and roast at 350°F (180°C) for about 5 minutes, or until tender. Check a few times while it's cooking to make sure that the asparagus does not overcook. Serve hot.

To serve, put 2 portobello caps on a plate, slice the cap in several pieces, fan it out and spoon some of the warmed red wine sauce over it. Place half of the mashed cauliflower and some of the cooked asparagus on the plate.

> note: You can sprinkle some nutritional yeast on top of the garlic mashed cauliflower to create a grated cheese appearance when you finish baking it.

Green Goddess Bowl

This delicious and eye-pleasing bowl is in the spirit of spring cleaning: getting your greens supercharges your body with nutrients, helps detoxify, boosts your immune system and cleanses your colon with plenty of healthy fiber. Bowls are a great option for easy weeknight suppers or quick healthy lunches. You can prep everything you need for a week full of healthy meals by cooking a big pot of quinoa, making your hummus and steaming or roasting your favorite vegetables. I've been dipping into this week's hummus as a snack with veggie chips all week. The greens we're focusing on here are kale, asparagus and broccoli. Oh, and there's a hint of radish in there for color. There's a lovely creamy green hummus on top, made from white beans and spinach. Avocado gives a nice serving of healthy, creamy plant-based fats to keep you satisfied for hours.

Serves 2

Green Hummus
3½ oz (100 g) fresh spinach

15 oz (425 g) white beans (canned or cooked)

2 cloves garlic

Zest and juice of 1 lemon

¼ cup (60 ml) olive oil

½ tsp salt

Pinch of freshly ground black pepper

Pinch of smoked paprika

Green Goddess Bowl
2 cups (91 g) broccoli florets

1 tbsp (15 ml) olive oil

8 spears asparagus, ends trimmed

2 cups (134 g) chopped kale

2 cups (370 g) cooked quinoa

1 avocado

2 radishes, sliced thinly, for garnish

¼ bunch (14 g) fresh cilantro, for garnish

½ tsp za'atar, for garnish (see Note)

For the hummus, bring a small pot of water to boil and submerge the spinach in the boiling water for about 10 seconds or until just wilted or blanched. Remove from the water and set aside. Save the water to steam your broccoli. In a food processor, combine the blanched spinach with the white beans, garlic, lemon zest, lemon juice, olive oil, salt, pepper and paprika and puree until smooth. Set aside until ready to use.

To make the goddess bowls, using the same boiling water in which you blanched the spinach, place the broccoli florets in a colander over the simmering water and cover with a lid. Steam until the florets are tender, for 5 to 7 minutes. In a skillet, heat the oil over medium heat. Add the asparagus spears to the skillet and cook until just browned and barely tender. In the last 3 minutes of cooking, add the kale to the pan and cook until the greens have wilted.

Heat the cooked quinoa and divide between two bowls. Slice the avocado in half, remove the pit and slice the flesh into slices lengthwise. Place half of the avocado in each bowl, as well as half the broccoli, asparagus and kale. Place a generous dollop of the green hummus in each bowl. Garnish each bowl with radish, cilantro and za'atar.

note: Za'atar is a Middle Eastern spice commonly made with dried thyme, oregano and marjoram and often includes dried sumac as well.

Celery Root, Mushroom and Sweet Potato Shepherd's Pie

A warming casserole like this is a good vehicle for root vegetables. Celery root (a.k.a. celeriac) is a totally unappreciated vegetable. It's pretty ugly! The skin is gnarly and I think that many people might be a little intimidated to approach it. The truth is, it can be cooked like almost any other root vegetable. It's dense and will hold up to long cooking, such as braising, long sautéing or boiling. It's simmered here with the mushrooms and other vegetables in the pie filling. The mushrooms give the dish a nice earthy flavor—I used shiitakes and button mushrooms, but you can sub any of your favorite mushrooms instead!

Serves 2 to 4

Celery Root and Mushroom Filling
2 tbsp (30 ml) melted coconut oil

1 small white onion, diced

2 cloves garlic, minced

1 cup (75 g) shiitake mushrooms, quartered

1 cup (75 g) button mushrooms, quartered

2 carrots, peeled and cut on the bias

3 celery ribs, sliced

1 celery root, peeled and cut into ½" (1.3-cm) cubes

¼ cup (60 ml) dry white wine

¼ tsp dried thyme

Salt and freshly ground black pepper

1 cup (236 ml) water, plus more as needed

1 tbsp (8 g) nutritional yeast

2 tsp (2 g) arrowroot powder

Mashed Sweet Potato Topping
2 large sweet potatoes, peeled

Salt and freshly ground black pepper

2 to 3 tbsp (30 to 45 ml) unsweetened almond milk (optional)

For the filling, in a medium saucepan, heat the coconut oil over very low heat and add the onion and garlic. Sauté for 3 minutes, or until the onion is translucent. Add the mushrooms, carrots, celery and celery root. Sauté until the vegetables are barely tender, for about 3 minutes. Add the white wine, thyme and salt and pepper and cook until the wine is reduced, about 5 minutes. Add the water, nutritional yeast and arrowroot powder. Bring to a simmer and cook 5 to 10 minutes until the mixture has thickened and the vegetables are tender. Set aside until ready to assemble the shepherd's pie.

For the sweet potato topping, place the sweet potatoes in a medium saucepan and fill with water to completely cover. Cook over low heat until tender to the center, 20 to 30 minutes. Drain and mash the sweet potatoes with a whisk (it's quite easy, actually) or electric hand mixer. Season with salt and pepper to taste and unsweetened almond milk, if desired.

To assemble, preheat the oven to 350°F (180°C). Place the filling in a 9-inch (23-cm) square baking dish. Top with a layer of the mashed sweet potato. Place the dish, uncovered, in the oven and bake for 15 to 20 minutes, or until the center is hot and the sweet potato topping is gently browned.

Freekeh Risotto

with Roasted Trumpet Mushrooms

Surprisingly creamy and easy to cook, this dish can be altered to use whatever vegetables are in season. Freekeh is a unique supergrain—it's basically wheat harvested when young and green. It has a chewy texture and a pleasant nutty flavor. It's been a staple of Middle Eastern cuisine for centuries. Definitely give it a try if it's available in your area. If you can't find it, you can substitute quinoa or rice with great results.

Serves 2 to 4

Freekeh
2 cups (473 ml) water

1 cup (185 g) cracked freekeh

Pinch of salt

Cashew Milk
½ cup (68 g) cashews, soaked in water for 2 hours, then drained and rinsed

1 cup (236 ml) water

Roasted Trumpet Mushrooms
4 large trumpet mushrooms, sliced lengthwise

1 tbsp (15 ml) olive oil, plus more for pan

Salt and freshly ground black pepper

Risotto
2 tbsp (30 ml) olive oil

2 medium leeks, washed and thinly sliced up to the green part of the leek

2 cloves garlic, minced

¼ cup (60 ml) white wine

Water, as needed

½ cup (118 ml) vegetable stock or water, plus more as needed

Pinch of dried thyme

1 small bunch living watercress (optional)

For the freekeh, in a saucepan, combine the water, freekeh and salt and cook, covered, over low heat for 20 to 30 minutes, or until the freekeh has absorbed the water and is tender (keep covered until all the water is absorbed). You can also cook this in a pressure cooker or rice cooker in the same manner as rice. You can cook the freekeh ahead and store in an airtight container for up to 5 days.

For the cashew milk, in a blender, combine the cashews and water and blend for 1 to 2 minutes. Refrigerate until ready to serve. No need to filter.

For the trumpet mushrooms, preheat the oven to 350°F (180°C). Toss the trumpet mushrooms in the olive oil and place them on a lightly oiled baking sheet. Season with salt and pepper. Roast for about 10 minutes, or until tender.

For the risotto, in a large skillet, heat the olive oil over low heat. Add the leeks and garlic and sauté for 2 to 3 minutes. Add the white wine and continue to sauté until the wine has cooked off. Add a little water, then cover and cook for 5 more minutes, or until the leeks are very soft. Add the cooked freekeh, cashew milk and vegetable stock and bring to a simmer. Add the dried thyme and cook until the risotto thickens and is creamy. To serve, portion the risotto into 2 bowls and garnish with the roasted mushrooms and watercress, if using. Add a little warm stock to the bowl around the risotto.

notes: You can substitute other grains for freekeh if you'd like—quinoa is especially delicious.

You can use store-bought nut milk instead of making your own.

Gluten-Free Mac and Cheese

This is a perfect weeknight supper—and the sauce makes a mean nacho! I do recommend using freshly made nut milk, rather than store-bought, in this particular recipe.

Serves 4

Mac and Cheese Sauce

1 cup (137 g) cashews

½ (4-oz [113-g]) bell pepper, seeded and chopped

2 tbsp (16 g) nutritional yeast flakes

1½ tsp (8 ml) cider vinegar

1½ tsp (8 g) sea salt

¼ cup (60 ml) water

1 tbsp (15 ml) olive oil

½ tsp ground turmeric

Cashew Milk

½ cup (69 g) cashews, soaked in water for 1 hour, then drained and rinsed

1 cup (236 ml) water

Pasta

1 tbsp (18 g) salt, plus more to taste

1 (8-oz [226-g]) package gluten-free elbow macaroni (I like Ancient Harvest Quinoa Elbows)

Olive oil

To Serve

Fresh herbs, such as flat-leaf parsley and thyme (optional)

For the mac and cheese sauce, in a blender, combine the cashews, bell pepper, nutritional yeast, vinegar, salt, water, olive oil and turmeric and puree for about 2 minutes, or until smooth. Set aside until ready to use.

To make the cashew milk, in a blender, combine the soaked cashews and water. Puree for about 30 seconds, or until the cashews are incorporated. Strain and discard the pulp.

To cook the pasta, fill a medium saucepan with water and bring to a boil. Add 1 tablespoon (18 g) of salt to the water and then add the gluten-free pasta. Cook for about 5 minutes, or until just al dente. Drain the pasta and rinse with cold water to stop the cooking. Drizzle a little olive oil and a pinch of salt over the pasta and toss until all the pasta is well coated.

In a saucepan, combine the blended sauce with ½ cup (120 ml) of the cashew milk. Heat slowly until the mixture begins to thicken and become creamy. Add more cashew milk, if necessary, to achieve your desired consistency. Cashew milk thickens very quickly when you cook with it, so be sure to keep an eye on your pot and keep the heat low. Add the cooked pasta to the heated sauce and cook for a few minutes, taking care to keep stirring occasionally and to prevent overcooking the pasta.

Serve topped with fresh herbs, if desired.

notes: You can mix in other ingredients, such as mushrooms, tomato, broccoli, spinach, etc. to give unique character to your dish. Truffle oil makes a delicious addition as well.

You can use store-bought nut milk instead of making your own, but I prefer homemade.

Body Ecology Bowl

Simple sautéed vegetables, greens and quinoa are healthy, nourishing and delicious with good-for-your-gut cultured vegetables. If you don't have the time to make them at home, you can use store-bought cultured vegetables, providing they are unpasteurized and raw. Incorporating cultured vegetables to your diet helps improve your digestion, nutrient absorption and immunity. Learning how to make your own at home is economical and even fun once you get the hang of it.

Serves 2 to 4

White Quinoa
2 cups (473 ml) water

1 cup (240 g) uncooked white quinoa

1 tsp salt

Sautéed Butternut Squash and Kale
1 tbsp (15 ml) melted coconut oil

¼ onion, sliced

1 clove garlic, minced

4 cups (892 g) butternut squash, peeled, seeded and diced

2 cups (150 g) kale or spinach

Pinch of salt

Freshly ground black pepper

Cultured Vegetables
1 head green cabbage, shredded

1 bunch kale, chopped very finely

5 or 6 collard leaves, chopped very finely

½ head cauliflower, broken in tiny florets

2 carrots, shredded

2 cloves garlic, peeled and minced

1 tbsp (7 g) celery seeds

1 tbsp (3 g) dried oregano

1½ tsp (1 g) dried basil

1 to 2 cups (236 to 473 ml) water, or more as needed

1 (1-oz [28-g]) culture starter (optional)

Outer cabbage leaves, for jars

To prepare the quinoa, in a saucepan, bring the water to a boil and add the quinoa. Cover, lower the heat and simmer for 20 minutes, or until all the water is absorbed. Season with the salt and fluff with a fork. Allow to stand, covered, for 5 minutes before serving.

For the sautéed squash and kale, heat the coconut oil in a skillet over low heat and sauté the onion and garlic until the onion is translucent, about 3 minutes. Toss in the squash and sauté until tender, about 8 minutes. Add kale at the very end of the cooking time, and cook until just wilted. Season with salt and pepper to taste.

To make the cultured vegetables, in a very large bowl, combine all the vegetables, seeds, and herbs. Transfer approximately one-quarter of the vegetable mixture to a blender. Add enough filtered water to the blender to create a brine the consistency of thick juice (see Note). Blend well, then add the culture starter (if using) to this brine. Pour the brine into the vegetable mixture in the large bowl. Mix together well. Pack the mixture down into as many pint- or quart-size (500-ml or 1-L) glass jars as necessary to hold all of the mixture, using a potato masher or your fist to pack vegetables very tightly. You want to force out most of the air. Leave about 2 inches (5 cm) of room at the top of each container for the vegetables to expand. Roll up several outer cabbage leaves into a tight log shape and place them on top to fill the remaining 2-inch (5-cm) space. Clamp each jar closed, or screw on its lid very tightly. Let the vegetables sit at approximately 70°F (21°C) or room temperature for at least a week. Two weeks may be even better. Refrigerate to slow down the fermentation. Fermented vegetables will keep in the fridge for many weeks, becoming softer and more delicious as time passes! Eat at least ¼ cup (56 g) of cultured vegetables with every meal.

To assemble the bowls, portion the quinoa into 2 to 4 separate bowls. Arrange some of the sautéed squash and kale on top of the quinoa in each bowl. Place 1 tablespoon (15 g) of cultured vegetables in each bowl. You can add fresh salad on the side, if desired.

note If your blender is small, you may have to make your cultured vegetables in two batches.

Lentil-Mushroom Soup

It's important to have an easy go-to soup that you can whip up for a stress-free lunch or dinner. Or better yet, make a double batch on a Sunday and let it nourish you all week. This soup is especially good to have on hand in the winter when you want something healthy and filling. Play around with the mushrooms you add, as each kind has a unique flavor.

Serves 4

1 tbsp (15 ml) melted coconut oil

2 cups (150 g) chopped mushrooms

½ cup (80 g) chopped onion

3 celery ribs, chopped

2 carrots, chopped

2 cloves garlic, minced

1 cup (200 g) dried green lentils

1 tsp cumin

1 sprig thyme

4 cups (946 ml) vegetable stock or water, plus more if needed

1 tsp gluten-free tamari, or to taste

Salt and freshly ground black pepper

Heat the coconut oil in a skillet over low heat and sauté the mushrooms, onion, celery, carrots and garlic for 2 to 3 minutes. Add the lentils, cumin, thyme and vegetable stock and bring to a boil. Simmer covered, until the lentils are done, for about 30 minutes, adding more vegetable stock while cooking if the soup becomes too thick. Add the tamari, salt and pepper to taste and enjoy!

Getting Your Greens

Nutrient-Packed Raw Salads, Soups and Appetizers

Salads, soups and appetizers are the lifeblood of a high raw lifestyle. They are extremely healthy, can be infinitely customized and are very fast. Even the busiest person can toss together a gourmet salad. Many ingredients can be prepared in advance and refrigerated to be combined and dressed in minutes just before eating. Here's an insider tip: The best way to dress a salad is to put the dressing on the bottom of a large bowl, put the vegetables on top of the dressing and toss. Especially with creamy dressings, this technique distributes that creamy goodness more evenly.

Raw soups are almost all blended, either entirely or partially. It may seem a little odd at first to serve soup lukewarm, but you can blend soups for 5 minutes and they will warm up gently, if you'd like to.

And finally, there's something festive and casual about appetizers. My guilt-free raw appetizers are ideal for entertaining, holidays and get-togethers. Try my Nachos with Bell Pepper Chips (page 101), Cucumber Spring Rolls (page 94) or Cauliflower-Chia Nori Rolls (page 97) for your next gathering. Get inspired to make your favorite cooked dishes in high raw style.

Cucumber Spring Rolls

Who doesn't love spring rolls? These are always a true crowd-pleaser. Full of bright, herby flavors and crisp, fresh textures, spring rolls are beautiful, satisfying and delicious. Not to mention versatile! Once you get the hang of rolling them, you can play around with the filling. I like to change up the vegetables for variety—try crunchy, colorful carrots and bell peppers or spicy chiles for a kick. Add some sriracha or other hot sauce to the dipping sauce if you like it hot.

Makes 1 roll

Marinated Shiitake Mushrooms
2 tsp (9 ml) agave nectar

4 tbsp (60 ml) gluten-free tamari

Pinch of red pepper flakes

Pinch of salt

4 shiitake mushrooms, sliced

Dipping Sauce
1 tsp agave nectar or pure maple syrup

1 tbsp (15 ml) gluten-free tamari

For Assembly
5 slices cucumber (sliced very thinly lengthwise on a mandoline slicer; see Note)

2 tbsp (5 g) roughly chopped fresh basil

2 tbsp (6 g) roughly chopped fresh mint

2 tbsp (5 g) roughly chopped fresh cilantro

¼ cup (85 g) finely shredded green or red cabbage

½ avocado, pitted, peeled and thinly sliced

Chopped scallions, for garnish

For the marinated mushrooms, in a bowl, whisk together the agave, tamari, red pepper flakes and salt and toss the sliced mushrooms in the marinade until thoroughly coated. Allow to sit for about 10 minutes so the marinade completely sinks in. Set aside.

For the dipping sauce, in a small bowl, whisk together the maple syrup and tamari. Set aside.

Lay the cucumber slices lengthwise, side by side, on a sushi mat to form a sheet. In the same way as making a sushi roll, layer the mushrooms, herbs, cabbage and avocado slices, one on top of one another, on the half of the laid-out cucumber closest to you on the sushi mat.

Using the sushi mat to compress the roll so it stays nice and firm, roll the cucumber slices around the filling to form a roll about 4 inches (10 cm) in length. Remove the roll from the sushi mat and carefully cut in half. You can also cut this roll into bite-size pieces. Serve with the dipping sauce, sprinkling the rolls and sauce with chopped scallions.

note   It's very pretty to layer the cucumber slices when making the rolls, but they can be hard to handle if you haven't sliced them thinly enough. They might not roll up very easily if they're too thick. The roll will tend to come apart and not stick to itself. Try to slice them as thinly as possible for the best results! But if you are having trouble getting them as thin as necessary to roll them up in a sheet, don't worry. You can use a single slice of cucumber to make a mini roll with no layering required!

Cauliflower-Chia Nori Rolls

This version of sticky rice is the best raw vegan replacement for traditional sushi rice. This cauliflower really resembles rice, has a very neutral flavor and sticks together with the help of the chia seeds, which also give an extra boost of protein and healthy fats. Feel free to change up the fillings: you can use any vegetables, such as broccoli, fennel and even sweet potato. Enjoy this naturally oil-free dish as a snack, or pair it with a light seaweed salad for a perfect lunch.

Makes 4 rolls

Sushi Rice

1 head cauliflower

2 tsp (6 g) chia seeds

1 tsp coconut sugar (optional, or use other unrefined sugar)

1 tsp salt

2 tsp (10 ml) cider vinegar

Sushi Roll

4 sheets sushi nori

2 cups (40 g) arugula or other greens

1 avocado, pitted, peeled and sliced into strips

2 medium tomatoes, seeded and cubed

1 red bell pepper, seeded and sliced into strips

1 cucumber, sliced into strips

2 green onions, sliced, plus more for garnish (optional)

1 jalapeño pepper, sliced

Sesame seeds, for garnish (optional)

Soy sauce, for dipping

For the sushi rice, cut the cauliflower head into florets, discard the stem and leaves, and place in a food processor. Pulse until the cauliflower is broken up into fine, rice-size pieces. Transfer to a mixing bowl. Add the chia, coconut sugar, salt and cider vinegar. Allow to sit for 10 to 15 minutes for the chia seeds to set before making the sushi rolls. Transfer the cauliflower to a clean dish towel and squeeze to remove some of the excess liquid. Your roll will be drier and last longer.

For each sushi roll, center one nori sheet on a bamboo sushi mat. First, spread a layer of the greens on the nori. Pressing down gently, spread a thin layer of the prepared cauliflower rice on the bed of greens, the full width of the nori, and press into a thin layer. Arrange one-quarter of the avocado, tomatoes, bell pepper, cucumber, green onions and jalapeño in a horizontal line down the center of the rice. Lift the end of the mat, and gently roll the layers into a "burrito," pressing firmly on the roll to compress the roll evenly. Wet the end of the nori before closing the roll, so it seals shut. Cut each roll into 4 to 6 slices, using a sharp knife.

To serve the sushi, place the cut rolls on a plate or board and garnish with sesame seeds and more green onions, if desired. Add a side of the soy sauce for dipping and eat with your fingers.

note   Squeezing the extra liquid out of the cauliflower rice is a very important step. It makes a huge difference in the quality of your roll.

Caponata is a Sicilian sweet-and-sour version of ratatouille, usually made with eggplant, but here I've substituted zucchini. It's meant to be served at room temperature, and I like it cold as well. A wonderful topping for bruschetta, as served here, it is also tasty with raw crudités. I like to add cashew cheese (page 65) as an additional topping to complement the caponata.

Serves 4 to 6

Caponata Dressing

2 tbsp (30 ml) fresh lemon juice

1 date, pitted and chopped

⅛ cup (19 g) sun-dried tomato, soaked in water for 1 hour, then rinsed

¼ tsp salt

1 tbsp (15 ml) olive oil

¼ cup (60 ml) water

Caponata

½ cup (60 g) diced red onion

1 cup (120 g) diced zucchini

¾ cup (80 g) seeded and diced red bell pepper

2 tbsp (27 g) golden raisins

2 tbsp (16 g) sunflower seeds

¼ cup (10 g) fresh basil, roughly chopped

2 tbsp (16 g) capers

1 cup (140 g) chopped tomato

Pinch of freshly ground black pepper

Bruschetta

1 recipe Buckwheat Flax Crust (page 25; see directions for how to shape)

6 to 8 sprigs fresh basil, for garnish

For the dressing, in a high-powered blender, combine the lemon juice, date, sun-dried tomato and salt and puree. When a chunky paste is formed, add the olive oil and water a little at a time until the mixture becomes thick. Set aside until ready to use. This dressing will keep refrigerated for up to 2 weeks in an airtight container.

For the caponata, in a bowl, combine the onion, zucchini, red bell pepper, golden raisins, sunflower seeds, basil, capers, tomato and black pepper and mix well. Toss with ½ cup (118 ml) of the caponata dressing, adding more dressing if desired.

To make the buckwheat crust, follow the crust recipe for Spinach, Leek and Sun-Dried Tomato Quiche (page 25), but instead of forming it into tarts, use an offset spatula to spread it into a ¼-inch (6-mm)-thick sheet on a solid dehydrator sheet or a piece of parchment paper. Score the raw cracker batter into cracker-size squares with the edge of your spatula. Dehydrate for 4 hours at 115°F (46°C), then flip crackers over and dehydrate another 4 hours. They should be easy to pull apart when they are done dehydrating.

To assemble the bruschetta, arrange the buckwheat crust on a board and top with a few spoonfuls of the caponata and garnish with fresh basil.

note   This mixture will separate and become watery if you dress it too soon before serving. It's best to make the caponata vegetable mix and dress it right before serving. If it does become watery, mix it well again until creamy.

Nachos
with Bell Pepper Chips

Kids will love these nachos, and they are naturally grain-free. You can replace fried tortilla chips with different fun vegetables—try jicama, raw cauliflower, cucumber and even roasted sweet potato. Let your kids join in to build the nachos and make it a party. Easy, cheesy.

Serves 4

Pico de Gallo

1 cup (150 g) chopped grape tomatoes

¼ cup (33 g) chopped red onion

¼ cup (10 g) fresh cilantro, chopped

Juice of 1 lime

1 jalapeño, chopped

Pinch of salt

Nacho Cheese

1 cup (137 g) cashews, soaked in water for 2 hours, then drained and rinsed

1 cup (124 g) seeded and chopped red bell pepper

2 tbsp (16 g) nutritional yeast

1½ tsp (8 ml) cider vinegar

1½ tsp (8 g) sea salt

¼ cup (60 ml) water

1 tbsp (15 ml) olive oil

½ tsp ground turmeric

To Assemble

3 bell peppers (1 yellow, 1 orange and 1 red), seeded and sliced into large pieces

1 ear of corn, shucked

1 (15-oz [425-g]) can black beans, drained (optional, since the beans are not raw)

¼ cup (60 ml) store-bought coconut yogurt

1 avocado, pitted, peeled and cut into pieces

1 jalapeño pepper, seeded and sliced

¼ cup (10 g) fresh cilantro, chopped

For the pico de gallo, add the grape tomatoes, red onion, cilantro, lime juice, jalapeño and salt to a mixing bowl. Toss until well combined.

For the nacho cheese, in a blender, combine the cashews, bell pepper, nutritional yeast, vinegar, sea salt, water, olive oil and turmeric. Blend until smooth and set aside until ready to use. This will keep for up to 7 days in an airtight container in your refrigerator.

To assemble the nachos, on a tray, spread out the sliced bell peppers like tortilla chips. Drizzle with the nacho cheese. Top with the corn kernels, black beans, pico de gallo, coconut yogurt, avocado, sliced jalapeño and cilantro. Add more nacho cheese, if desired. Serve immediately.

> *note* This cheese sauce has a shelf life of 7 days. Make a big batch and keep it around for all kinds of delicious snacks.

Warm Asparagus

with Avocado Hollandaise, Chive Oil and Radish

I love to use my dehydrator in the winter to lightly soften all kinds of vegetables and serve them warm. Asparagus is best only lightly cooked anyway, so it's a perfect vegetable to prepare in this manner. I also use my dehydrator to prepare mushrooms, broccoli, cauliflower, green beans and peppers in the same way. The length of time in the dehydrator will vary according to the vegetable and how thick the pieces are—larger pieces take longer, naturally. If you don't have a dehydrator, just roast the vegetables for the shortest possible time to achieve the desired tenderness. Try this as a savory brunch dish!

Serves 2

Avocado Hollandaise

1 medium ripe avocado, peeled, pitted and sliced

Juice of 1 large lemon (about 3 tbsp [45 ml])

Pinch of cayenne pepper

¼ tsp kosher salt, plus more to taste

⅛ tsp ground white pepper, plus more to taste

¼ to ½ cup (60 to 118 ml) warm water

Chive Oil

¼ cup (63 ml) olive oil

½ bunch chives

½ tsp salt

Warm Asparagus

1 bunch asparagus, washed, ends trimmed

2 or 3 radishes, sliced very thinly

Salt and freshly ground black pepper

For the avocado hollandaise, in a blender, combine the avocado, lemon juice, cayenne, salt, pepper and ¼ cup (60 ml) of the water. Puree until smooth, drizzling in additional water as needed to create a smooth, pourable consistency. Taste and add additional salt and pepper if desired. If you want a warmer avocado hollandaise, you can heat it gently in a small pan over low heat, stirring frequently until warm, about 5 minutes. Add a little more water, if needed. This keeps refrigerated in an airtight container for 2 to 3 days.

For the chive oil, in a blender, combine the olive oil, chives and salt and puree for 1 to 2 minutes. Strain and store in a jar or bottle. This is a tasty finishing oil to drizzle on top of vegetables or salads.

To make the warm asparagus, toss the asparagus spears with a little bit of the chive oil. Place on a dehydrator sheet and dehydrate for 1 hour at 118°F (48°C). If you don't have a dehydrator, place them on a baking sheet and roast at 250°F (121°C) for 10 minutes. When ready, place on a serving platter and dress with ½ cup (75 g) of the avocado hollandaise, radish, salt and pepper. Drizzle with more chive oil and serve.

Cauliflower Samosas

with Mango Chile Chutney and Cucumber Raita

Looking for a healthy snack that travels well? Try these scrumptious samosas with two delicious dipping sauces. The spices give an extra flavor boost as well as being great for your health.

Makes 8 samosas

Cauliflower Samosas

¼ cup (31 g) walnuts, soaked 2 hours in filtered water, then drained and rinsed

¼ head cauliflower, stemmed and cut into florets

¼ sweet potato, peeled and chopped

¼ cup (27 g) very finely minced onion

¼ cup (45 g) peeled and grated zucchini

1 tbsp (20 g) frozen green peas, defrosted

1 clove garlic, peeled and minced

1 tbsp (7 g) ground flaxseeds

1½ tsp (3 g) chopped fresh cilantro

1½ tsp (7 ml) melted coconut oil

¼ tbsp (3 g) curry powder

¼ tsp ground cinnamon

¼ tsp ground coriander

Pinch of chili powder

¼ tsp ground turmeric

1 tsp fresh lemon juice

Pinch of sea salt

Mango Chile Chutney

1 cup (251 g) chopped mango

1 tbsp (15 ml) agave nectar

2 tbsp (30 ml) cider vinegar

½ small Thai chile or jalapeño pepper, seeded and finely diced

1 (1" [2.5-cm]) piece fresh ginger, peeled and grated

1 clove garlic, peeled and minced

¼ tsp ground coriander

1 tbsp (6 g) chopped fresh mint

¼ tsp salt, or to taste

Cucumber Raita

1 cup (129 g) cashews, soaked in water overnight, then drained and rinsed

¼ cup (60 ml) fresh lemon juice

1 tbsp (15 ml) agave nectar

Up to ¼ cup (60 ml) water (optional)

1 cucumber, peeled, grated and squeezed

2 tbsp (6 g) chopped fresh mint

Pinch of ground cumin

Pinch of salt

For the samosas, in a food processor, combine the walnuts, cauliflower and sweet potato and puree until smooth. Transfer to a bowl and mix well with the onion, zucchini and peas. Add the remaining samosa ingredients and mix until a dough is formed. Form into balls (or pyramids, as I have in the picture on page 104). Dehydrate on nonstick sheets for 2 to 4 hours at 115°F (46°C).

For the chutney, in a bowl, toss all the chutney ingredients together and allow to marinate for 2 hours or overnight. Transfer the mixture to a blender and pulse to create a chunky texture. Keep refrigerated until ready to use.

For the raita, in a blender, combine the cashews, lemon juice and agave and blend until smooth. Add water, if necessary, to thin. Transfer to a bowl and toss with the cucumber and mint. Season with the cumin and salt to taste.

To serve, warm the samosas gently in your dehydrator at 115°F (46°C) or in the oven for about 15 minutes at 250°F (121°C) and serve with a side of the chutney and raita for dipping. I prefer these a little warm for the best texture.

Cucumber-Coconut Bisque

with Chili and Lime

This velvety soup is amazing in the summertime. You can add a little more cayenne if you like it spicy. Also, this soup is very hydrating and will help keep your skin looking smooth and glowing in the hot summer months. The cucumber is smoothing, while the coconut contains beneficial fats and has a deliciously creamy texture. This bisque reminds me of similar chilled soups I have had that were made with yogurt.

Serves 2

1 cup (122 g) young Thai coconut meat

1 large cucumber, peeled

1½ cups (355 ml) filtered water

Juice of 1 lime

Pinch of salt

Pinch of freshly ground black pepper

Pinch of cayenne pepper

Chopped green onion, for garnish

Olive oil, for garnish

For the soup, in a blender, combine the coconut meat, cucumber, water and lime juice and blend until smooth. Strain the soup through a fine-mesh strainer and season with salt, pepper and cayenne. Chill for 1 hour before serving. Garnish with green onion and a drizzle of olive oil.

note   Young Thai coconut has a few great uses: The water is delicious, and the meat can be added to smoothies and soups. The meat freezes extremely well, so if you have coconuts that you're opening for the water, don't throw away the meat. Opening the coconuts can be a little bit tricky, so I recommend watching a few videos online before attempting it for the first time. I use a cleaver and carefully cut off the top by piercing all around the top of the coconut and then popping off the top with the heel of my knife. Once you empty out the water, you can scoop out the meat with a spoon and then rinse it off under some cool water.

Celery-Apple Gazpacho

with Slivered Almonds

Jam-packed with natural sweetness, this fruity soup is so quick to make and refreshing in any season.

Serves 2

8 celery ribs

1 Granny Smith apple, cored

1½ cups (355 ml) cold water

2 tbsp (30 ml) olive oil, plus more for garnish

1 tbsp (15 ml) fresh lemon juice

1 tsp salt, plus more to taste

2 tbsp (14 g) slivered almonds, for garnish

Thinly sliced slivers of celery and celery leaves, for garnish

½ cup (75 g) diced apple, for garnish

In a blender, combine the celery, apple, water, olive oil, lemon juice and salt and blend until smooth. Strain through a sieve and allow to chill for 1 hour before serving. Garnish with slivered almonds, pieces of sliced celery, celery leaves, diced apple and olive oil.

Miso Soup

Miso soup was one of the first healthy things I learned to cook. This method for preparing it is a little untraditional, but it also preserves its healing properties. Serve it as a starter for any of the raw entrées in this book or make it the star of a light meal.

Serves 2

2 tbsp (30 ml) organic miso

2 cups (473 ml) hot water

1 tbsp (15 ml) gluten-free tamari

1 tbsp (6 g) grated fresh ginger

1 tsp salt (optional)

½ cup (35 g) sliced shiitake mushrooms

¼ cup (25 g) sliced scallion

¼ cup (33 g) very thinly sliced carrot

¼ cup (17 g) shredded kale

In a blender, combine the miso, hot water, tamari, grated ginger and salt, if desired, and puree until smooth. Pour the hot miso broth into 2 bowls and fill each bowl with half the mushrooms, scallion, carrot and kale.

note This is not technically raw, since the water is hot. You can make it any temperature you choose, but I like to use boiling water, as I find that it starts cooling off quickly, but stays hot enough to make a satisfying raw soup in the winter.

Cream of Watercress Soup

This creamy green soup is truly high raw. Only certain ingredients are cooked to bring out the flavors, and the rest are kept raw to maximize their nutritional integrity. Serve either chilled or barely warmed.

Serves 2 to 4

2 tbsp (30 ml) olive oil

1 large onion, chopped

1 celery rib with leaves

1 small ancho chile (optional)

2 cups (68 g) packed watercress leaves

1 tbsp (15 ml) gluten-free tamari

2¼ cups (530 ml) unsweetened almond milk

1 tbsp (15 ml) coconut cream

½ tsp ground white pepper

⅛ tsp cayenne pepper

Salt

In a medium saucepan, heat the olive oil over medium-low heat. Add the onion and sauté for 2 to 3 minutes, or until translucent and soft. Transfer the onion to a blender and add the celery, ancho chile (if using), watercress, tamari, almond milk, coconut cream, white pepper, cayenne and salt. Puree until smooth. You can chill this soup and serve it like a vichyssoise, or you can heat it gently before serving.

Cream of Mushroom Soup

If you have grown up eating the canned version of this soup made with cow's milk and tons of salt, you are going to really love this healthier version. So creamy and earthy tasting. If you have a high-speed blender, blend this soup for a few minutes to warm it up gently, as the friction from the blender has a warming effect. You can also heat the water up before blending. If you do use hot water, be sure to get a kitchen towel to cover the blender lid; start at the lowest speed and gradually increase it.

Serves 4

1½ cups (355 ml) water

1½ cups (105 g) mushrooms

¼ cup (34 g) pine nuts or cashews

½ small avocado, pitted and peeled

¼ cup (33 g) chopped red onion

1 clove garlic

½ tsp fresh thyme

½ tsp salt

Pinch of ground nutmeg

¼ tsp ground black pepper

In a blender, combine all the ingredients and puree until everything is well combined. Adjust the salt and pepper to taste.

note: Garnish with extra sliced mushrooms, fresh chopped red onions or freshly ground black pepper.

Whole Little Gem lettuce is so pretty as a salad, but you can also serve this with regular chopped romaine. Little Gem lettuce is baby romaine. Try grilling the lettuce for an added dimension of flavor. The ever-popular traditional Caesar salad is made with egg, anchovy and cheese, but with this vegan version, I can promise you'll never miss those ingredients.

Serves 2

Caesar Dressing

⅓ cup (52 g) cashews

1 tbsp (15 ml) cider vinegar

1 clove garlic

⅓ cup (79 ml) water

⅛ tsp freshly ground black pepper

1 tsp nutritional yeast

¾ tsp dark miso

⅛ cup (30 ml) olive oil

Salt

Little Gem Caesar Salad

2 to 4 whole heads Little Gem lettuce

2 small ripe avocados, pitted, peeled and chopped

2 to 3 radishes, thinly sliced

1 tbsp (8 g) nutritional yeast, for garnish

To make the dressing, in a blender, combine the cashews, vinegar, garlic, water, pepper, nutritional yeast and miso. Begin blending until smooth and then start slowly adding the olive oil. Add all the oil and blend until everything is fully incorporated, thick and creamy. Season with salt to taste. Store in a jar in your refrigerator for up to 2 weeks.

To build the salad, wash the lettuce, leaving the heads whole. Pat them dry gently with a clean dish towel or paper towel, then cut them in half lengthwise. Put 2 halves on each of 2 plates and dress with the Caesar dressing. Top the lettuce with one-quarter of the avocado and radish and a sprinkle of nutritional yeast.

Summer Corn Succotash

Most people don't eat corn raw, but it's absolutely delicious and a real treat in the summer when it's in season. No laborious prep required for this, so it's the perfect salad to make when you're short on time. This five-minute salad is delicious with a chilled soup or a fruity agua fresca for a refreshing raw meal. I also think it would be a great addition to a summer picnic. Try adding a pinch of spice if you like it hot, or toss with a little vegan mayo if you prefer a creamier salad.

Serves 2

1 ear of fresh sweet corn, shucked

½ zucchini, chopped

1 green onion, chopped

½ red bell pepper, chopped

½ green bell pepper, chopped

½ cup (85 g) halved grape tomatoes

1 small avocado, pitted, peeled and chopped

1 clove garlic, minced

2 tbsp (30 ml) fresh lime juice

1 tbsp (15 ml) olive oil

¼ tsp sea salt

Pinch of freshly ground black pepper

Pinch of cayenne pepper (optional)

2 cups (40 g) lightly packed arugula

2 tbsp (5 g) chopped fresh cilantro

In a mixing bowl, combine the corn kernels, zucchini, green onion, bell peppers, grape tomatoes, avocado and garlic. Toss well to mix. In a separate bowl, whisk together the lime juice, olive oil, sea salt and black pepper. Add the cayenne, if desired. Dress the salad with the dressing and toss once again. Serve on a bed of arugula, garnished with the cilantro.

Tangerine, Grapefruit and Avocado Salad

with **Arugula** and **Lemon Poppy Seed Vinaigrette**

Grapefruit is a valuable addition to any cleanse or raw detox: it's full of water, which helps flush the kidneys and liver, and there are abundant fat-burning enzymes that will boost your metabolism. Like lemon, it's considered an alkaline food even though it tastes acidic. Whether you juice them, eat them in salad or even grill them, you'll love these Ruby Reds.

Serves 2

Lemon Poppy Seed Vinaigrette

¼ cup (50 g) pitted and chopped dates

¼ cup (60 ml) fresh lemon juice

¼ cup (60 ml) water

½ tsp mustard powder

1 tsp minced red onion

⅓ cup (80 ml) olive oil

1½ tsp (4 g) poppy seeds

Salad

4 cups (80 g) arugula

4 tangerines, peeled, seeded and segmented

5 or 6 grapefruit segments, preferably Ruby Red

1 avocado, pitted, peeled and chopped

For the vinaigrette, in a blender, combine the dates, lemon juice, water, mustard powder and red onion. Puree, then add the oil slowly and blend until emulsified. After the olive oil is incorporated, mix in the poppy seeds by hand.

Toss with the arugula, then lay the tangerine and grapefruit segments and avocado on top.

Waldorf Salad

In this version of the classic Waldorf, fatty mayonnaise is replaced by healthy coconut yogurt, which will give you a probiotic boost. The salad makes a perfect lunch on the go, because the hearty ingredients hold up well for hours. Try to use organic produce if possible, since you're eating the skins of the apples and grapes.

Serves 2

6 tbsp (89 ml) plain coconut yogurt (see page 30 for homemade, or use store-bought)

1 tbsp (15 ml) fresh lemon juice

½ tsp salt

Pinch of freshly ground black pepper

2 cups (110 g) bitter lettuce mix, leaves torn

1 sweet apple, cored and chopped into matchsticks

1 cup (192 g) red seedless grapes, sliced in half, or ¼ cup (35 g) raisins

¼ cup (36 g) thinly sliced celery

¼ cup (50 g) chopped walnuts (optional: slightly toast them for a flavor boost)

4 sprigs fresh flat-leaf parsley

In a bowl, whisk together the coconut yogurt, lemon juice, salt and pepper. Set aside.

Arrange the lettuce on a platter. Add the apple, grapes and celery. Spoon the coconut yogurt dressing over the salad. Top the salad with the walnuts and parsley.

Rainbow Chopped Salad

I'm sure you've heard the saying to "eat the rainbow." The more color in your food, the greater the variety of nutrients. This hearty salad is practically a whole meal on its own. Whenever I eat a salad as a meal, I like to make sure there is plenty of crunch and texture and a little something fatty, like avocado. That variety is what makes this salad so satisfying and energizing.

Serves 2

Avocado Chili Lime Dressing

1 large avocado, pitted, peeled and sliced

2 tbsp (30 ml) fresh lime juice

½ tsp sea salt

Pinch of chili powder

½ cup (118 ml) water

½ cup (20 g) fresh cilantro

½ cup (30 g) fresh parsley

Chopped Salad

2 cups (110 g) greens (such as arugula, spinach or baby kale), chopped

1 cup (128 g) julienned carrot

1 cup (200 g) grape tomato, sliced

1 small beet, peeled and shredded

1 avocado, peeled, pitted and sliced

1 cup (133 g) cucumber, sliced

1 cup (40 g) fresh cilantro, stemmed

1 yellow bell pepper, seeded and sliced

¼ cup (32 g) pumpkin seeds

For the dressing, in a blender, combine all the dressing ingredients and blend until smooth. Store in an airtight container for up to 2 days.

To make the salad, in a mixing bowl, dress the greens with some of the dressing. Divide the greens between 2 bowls. Divide the rest of the vegetables between the 2 bowls, arranging them decoratively on top of the greens. Top with the pumpkin seeds and more dressing.

Niçoise Salad

with Sunflower "Tuna" Pâté

The vegan tuna salad in this recipe is a very satisfying lunch and travels well. It also is great in sandwiches, if you eat bread. The dulse is a mild sea vegetable that gives the pâté its tuna flavor. You can buy dulse in health food stores or Asian markets or even online. You will find that sprinkling dulse on your food will let you use less salt in your food because of the natural salinity of sea vegetables.

Serves 2

"Tuna" Pâté
½ cup (150 g) raw hulled sunflower seeds, soaked in water for 1 hour, then drained and rinsed well

1 cup (130 g) shredded carrot

¼ cup (15 g) fresh parsley, chopped

2 tbsp (30 ml) olive oil (optional)

1 tbsp (15 ml) fresh lemon juice

1 tbsp (15 ml) gluten-free tamari

1 tbsp (3 g) dulse flakes or kelp powder

Salt and freshly ground black pepper

Herb Vinaigrette
¼ cup (60 ml) olive oil

2 tbsp (30 ml) fresh lemon juice

1 shallot, minced

1 tsp dried thyme

1 tsp dried oregano

1 tsp stone-ground or Dijon mustard

Pinch of salt

Pinch of freshly ground black pepper

Niçoise Salad
4 oz (113 g) mâche (or other greens)

1 cup (178 g) cherry tomatoes, halved

½ cup (55 g) black olives, pitted

1 cup (125 g) string beans or haricots verts, washed and trimmed

1 small bunch (204 g) asparagus, ends trimmed

4 radishes

For the "tuna" pâté, in a food processor, pulse the soaked sunflower seeds until ground to a tunalike texture. Transfer to a mixing bowl and add the carrot, parsley, olive oil, lemon juice, tamari and dulse. Mix well and season to taste with salt and black pepper.

For the vinaigrette, in a small bowl or cup, whisk together the vinaigrette ingredients by hand.

On a platter, arrange the mâche into a bed, topped with the tomatoes, olives, string beans, asparagus, radishes and a ½-cup (120-g) scoop of the "tuna" pâté. Drizzle with some of the herb vinaigrette.

The remaining "tuna" pâté will keep for 1 week refrigerated.

The River of Life

Healthy Juices and Smoothies

Juices and smoothies are a daily staple for most raw vegans I know. So nutrient dense, so easy to digest and so fast to make. I think it's important to incorporate one of these beverages every day. You can replace meals easily with them, especially if you are trying to lose weight or are pursuing a detox program.

Meal replacement with healthy juices and smoothies is one of the best ways to increase the amount and variety of nutrients in your diet. Juices are packed with so much more nutrition than we normally get in a single meal because of the sheer volume of mineral-packed produce used to make them. Smoothies can be given nutrition boosts by adding whatever supplements you desire, such as vegan protein powder, omega fats or any number of incredible superfoods.

Green Forever Smoothie

I turn to this as my daily green smoothie. I prefer something less sweet in the morning and love to really pile on the greens. Don't be afraid of the cayenne and cinnamon—they really add a kick and are very healthy spices to add to any smoothie.

Serves 1

¼ cup (60 ml) coconut water or filtered water

2 heaping cups (134 g) kale

1 cup (67 g) chopped romaine lettuce

1 large celery rib, chopped

¼ green apple, cored and chopped

½ banana, peeled

¼ cup (52 g) chopped cucumber

¼ cup (10 g) fresh cilantro, chopped

¼ cup (15 g) fresh parsley, chopped

Juice of ¼ lemon

Pinch of cayenne pepper

Pinch of ground cinnamon

Pinch of ground turmeric

½ cup (70 g) ice, if desired

In a blender, combine all the ingredients and puree until smooth. Keep refrigerated for up to 1 day until ready to drink, although it's best to consume immediately.

Liquid Sunshine Smoothie

A powerfully anti-inflammatory treat. The bright notes of citrus are mellowed by the creamy flavors of maca, banana and coconut. If you would like to make this less sweet, replace the banana with half an avocado! It will be just as creamy and smooth.

Serves 1

In a blender, combine all the ingredients and puree until smooth. Serve immediately.

1 tbsp (4 g) ground chia seeds

¼ cup (60 ml) chilled unsweetened coconut water or filtered water

2 tbsp (30 ml) unsweetened coconut milk

1½ cups (190 g) orange segments (from 2 oranges)

1 (½" [1.3-cm]) piece fresh turmeric, peeled and roughly chopped, or 1 tsp ground

1 (1" [3-cm]) piece fresh ginger, peeled and grated

¼ tsp vanilla extract

1 banana

1 cup (140 g) ice

1 tsp agave nectar, maple syrup or stevia (optional)

1 tsp maca powder (optional)

Chunky Monkey Smoothie

Peanut butter and chocolate are a classic combination. Besides being delicious, these flavors will complement your favorite protein powder, and you'll also get a protein boost from the peanut butter. You can make this with almond butter if you don't like peanuts.

Serves 1

1 cup (236 ml) almond milk

2 frozen bananas, chopped

2 large fresh dates, pitted and chopped

1 tbsp (7 g) raw cacao powder

2 tbsp (32 g) peanut butter

1 tbsp (5 g) protein powder

1 cup (140 g) ice

In a blender, combine all the ingredients and puree until smooth. Serve immediately.

Piña Greenlada Smoothie

This is a green smoothie that kids will love. Naturally sweet and refreshing, tropical fruit is full of antioxidants, and coconut milk yields the creamiest texture imaginable. Play with the greens you use—any neutral-tasting greens will go well in this tropical concoction.

Serves 1

1 banana

½ cup (82 g) pineapple

½ cup (82 g) mango

¼ cup (60 ml) coconut milk, plus more as needed

5 leaves (200 g) chard, spinach or similar dark green

½ tsp vanilla extract

1 cup (240 g) ice

Shredded coconut, for garnish

In a blender, combine the banana, pineapple, mango and coconut milk and puree until smooth. Then, add the chard, vanilla and ice and blend until thick and creamy. Serve immediately, topped with shredded coconut.

note: It's fine to use frozen fruit if you'd like! Just reduce the ice or add a little more coconut milk, if necessary.

Wake Up Bulletproof Smoothie

If you add a little fat (such as the almond butter and coconut oil in this recipe) to your morning smoothie, you'll find that you have more sustained energy throughout the day. The fat slows absorption of the sugars in the date and banana, keeping you feeling full and satisfied for hours. This tastes like a mocha coffee drink, but is so much healthier.

Serves 1

¼ cup (60 ml) cold-brewed coffee

¼ cup (63 ml) almond milk

1 tbsp (15 ml) melted coconut oil

2 tbsp (32 g) almond butter

1 banana

1 tbsp (7 g) raw cacao powder

2 dates, pitted

½ cup (70 g) ice

In a blender, combine all the ingredients and puree until smooth. Serve immediately.

note If you would like to go sugar-free with this smoothie, skip the dates and banana and add half an avocado!

Aloe Margarita

The health benefits of aloe vera are numerous, beginning with improving the digestive system and strengthening the immune system. Aloe vera has been known to help delay the aging process, cure dermatitis and heal wounds. You can enjoy these benefits by drinking the juice of the aloe vera plant, which is readily available in health food stores. Try this much healthier nonalcoholic version of a margarita with your chips and dip.

Serves 2

2 tbsp (30 ml) aloe vera juice

¼ cup (60 ml) fresh lime juice

1 cup (236 ml) romaine lettuce, juiced

1 tbsp (15 ml) agave nectar, or stevia to taste

2 cups (280 g) ice

In a blender, combine the aloe, lime juice, romaine juice and agave and puree until smooth. Pour into margarita glasses over ice and serve.

note Garnish the margarita glasses with a sea salt rim and serve with lime wedges if you want to make it extra festive.

Watermelon Agua Fresca

In the dog days of summer, this is one of the most refreshing beverages you can make. Agua fresca means "fresh water." Watermelon is 92 percent water and is a perfectly delicious way to stay hydrated.

Serves 4

6 cups (912 g) sliced watermelon

¼ cup (60 ml) filtered fresh lime juice

1 cup (240 g) ice

In a blender, combine all the ingredients and puree until smooth. Serve immediately.

note: If you want to serve this later, leave the ice out of the recipe and blend only the watermelon and lime juice. Chill and serve over ice.

Cucumber-Mint Agua Fresca

Cucumber is an unusual ingredient to find in a sweet recipe, especially a beverage, but it really works. In this recipe, it tastes a little like a super smooth and refreshing limeade. The hint of mint is a great touch that gives an undertone of refreshing complexity.

Serves 2 to 4

1 cucumber

¼ cup (60 ml) fresh lime juice

2 tbsp (30 ml) agave nectar

2½ cups (591 ml) water

¼ cup (4 g) fresh mint leaves, plus more for garnish

Wash, peel and chop the cucumber. I recommend peeling because when you blend cucumber skin into the agua fresca it tends to create a slightly bitter taste. In a blender, combine the cucumber, lime juice, agave, water and mint and puree until smooth. Place in your refrigerator to chill for 1 hour. Serve over ice and stir before serving. Garnish with mint leaves.

Go-with-the-Flow Juice

In the same family as spinach and chard, beets are packed with vitamins, minerals, antioxidants and fiber. They are also high in vitamins C and B$_6$, folate, manganese, betaine and potassium. Beets have powerful antioxidant, anti-inflammatory and detoxification properties. It just takes a little bit of beet in this brightly hued juice to make a big health impact—and taste great.

Serves 1

4 carrots

6 celery ribs

½ beet

½ cucumber

3 beet leaves

Juice of 1 lemon (¼ cup [60 ml])

Wash all the produce very well (especially the beet!) and cut into pieces small enough to fit through the juicer chute. Juice all the produce in your juicer and serve immediately.

Fields of Green Juice

Juicing will supercharge your diet with nutrients. This recipe is one you can have anytime due to its low sugar content. Green apples are a good substitute for sweet apples when you are trying to cut down on sweet fruits. Also, the kale, romaine, cilantro and parsley are all helpful for boosting immunity and helping to detoxify your system.

Serves 1

3 romaine lettuce leaves

3 kale leaves

1 handful (20 g) fresh cilantro

1 handful (30 g) fresh parsley

4 celery ribs

1 cucumber

½ green bell pepper, seeded

1 lemon

1 green apple

Wash all the produce and cut into pieces large enough to fit into the chute of your juicer. Process all the ingredients in your juicer and serve immediately.

Ayurvedic Elixir Juice

The fruits and vegetables in this juice are highly effective blood purifiers and help increase red blood cell production and circulation, combat fatigue, increase energy and maintain healthy iron levels in the blood. That increase in oxygen in your blood will make you feel great! Grapefruit is an excellent blood purifier because the pectin fiber binds to heavy metals and cholesterol circulating in your system, thus cleansing your blood.

Serves 1

2 small carrots

1 cucumber

1 cup (165 g) peeled and roughly chopped fresh pineapple

1 grapefruit, peeled and segmented

2 oranges, peeled and segmented

¼ cup (24 g) fresh mint leaves

¼ cup (60 ml) coconut water/juice (optional)

Wash the carrots and cucumber and roughly chop in small enough pieces to fit in your juicer chute. Juice the carrots, cucumber, pineapple, grapefruit and orange segments in a juicer, throwing in the mint leaves at the end. Pour into a cup and mix with the coconut water, if desired. Serve immediately

Guilt-Free Indulgence

Raw Vegan Desserts

I have always thought of dessert as a gateway food for those wanting to try vegan cuisine. Most people experience sweet cravings, but even the most hardened junk food junkie can't take issue with chocolate, fruit, nuts and coconut. Whenever I get a chance to share raw vegan food with people new to this lifestyle, the desserts are always the things that disappear first!

In fact, most people won't even realize (and will be thrilled to learn) that there are nutritional benefits to raw vegan desserts! Free of processed sugar, flour and artery-clogging butter, these desserts are all naturally gluten-free as well. Made from whole foods, many are also Paleo.

Having any of these recipes on hand will be a lifesaver when you have cravings for something sweet. They all freeze well, too, so you don't have to worry about eating the whole thing at once.

Key Lime Pie

with Pistachio-Date Crust

Key lime pie is a traditional American dessert that I have reimagined as a raw vegan treat—minus the eggs, cream and processed sugar. Sweet!

Serves 6 to 8

Pistachio Date Crust

2 cups (340 g) raw pistachios

8 to 10 Medjool dates, pitted and chopped

½ tsp salt

1 tsp ground cinnamon

Key Lime Filling

1¼ cups (354 ml) unfiltered melted extra virgin coconut oil

18 oz (510 g) avocado flesh (about 3 avocados, depending on size)

1 cup (236 g) fresh Key lime juice from 6 to 9 Key limes

1½ cups (355 ml) light agave nectar

2 tbsp (15 g) soy lecithin granules

1 tsp vanilla extract

For the pistachio date crust, prepare an 8- or 9-inch (20.5- or 23-cm) springform pan by wrapping the bottom of the pan with plastic wrap to help the pie release. In a food processor, pulse the pistachios until the nuts are broken up and crumbly. Add the dates, salt and cinnamon to the processor and pulse until the mixture is fully incorporated and sticks together when compressed in your hand; it should not fall apart. If the mixture is still too dry, add a teaspoon of water to the mixture and pulse a few more times. When ready, press the mixture evenly into the bottom of the prepared pan. Spread evenly and firmly.

For the Key lime filling, gently melt the coconut oil until it liquefies. In a food processor, combine the avocado flesh with the lime juice, agave, soy lecithin and vanilla. Puree until the mixture is smooth. Add the melted coconut oil and process for about 2 more minutes, or until all the avocado chunks are blended into the mixture. Pour into the prepared crust and refrigerate overnight or until firm all the way through.

notes Many raw desserts use a springform pan, which lets you remove the pie very easily from the pan once it's set up. Springform pans can be bought at kitchen supply stores. However, you can still make this pie in a regular pie pan, if you don't have a springform on hand. Just make sure you double the crust recipe if using a regular pie pan, so you can make the crust go up the sides of the pan.

It's important to use only unfiltered coconut oil for this recipe so it sets up completely! Also, try to get light agave so you have a nice, light green color. Darker sweeteners, such as maple syrup or dark agave, will muddy the color, but will still taste good.

Soy lecithin is a healthy fat supplement that is available in health food stores. It acts as an emulsifier and helps the pie set up.

Lemon-Lavender Blueberry Cheesecake

Lavender is such a lovely and fragrant herb. Oh, you will love the way your house smells like a spa when you make this dessert!

This culinary herb can be used much like rosemary: It complements both sweet and savory dishes. The leaves can be used in cooking, but most of the essential oils are found in the blossoms, which have a subtly sweet, citrus flavor.

When blueberries are in season, they pair nicely with lavender, and of course share a lovely purplish-blue hue. This dessert is a lovely and healthy dish that will please everyone!

Serves 8–12

Walnut Date Crust

2 cups (250 g) walnuts

6 large dates, pitted and chopped

1 tsp ground cinnamon

½ tsp sea salt

Lemon Cheesecake Layer

2 cups (274 g) cashews, soaked in water for 2 hours, then drained and rinsed

1½ cups (120 g) peeled, pitted and chopped apple

1 cup (236 ml) melted coconut oil

1 cup (236 ml) pure maple syrup

½ cup (118 ml) fresh lemon juice

1 tsp vanilla extract

1 tbsp plus 1 tsp (11 g) nutritional yeast

1 tbsp (8 g) soy lecithin granules

1½ tsp (8 g) sea salt

For the crust, in a food processor, pulse the walnuts until the nuts are broken into fine pieces. Add the dates, cinnamon and sea salt. Pulse some more until the mixture begins to stick together. Line a 12-inch (30.5-cm) springform pan or pie pan with plastic wrap. Press the walnut mixture into the prepared pan.

For the lemon cheesecake layer, in a blender, combine all the ingredients for the lemon layer and blend well until smooth. Taste and adjust with more maple syrup, salt and lemon juice, if desired. Pour into the prepared crust and refrigerate for about 30 minutes, or until it begins to set.

(continued)

Lemon–Lavender Blueberry Cheesecake (continued)

Lavender-Blueberry Cheesecake Layer

2 cups (274 g) cashews, soaked for 2 hours, then drained and rinsed

1½ cups (120 g) peeled, seeded and chopped apple

1 cup (236 ml) melted coconut oil

1 cup (236 ml) pure maple syrup

½ cup (118 ml) pure lemon juice

1 tsp vanilla extract

1 tbsp plus 1 tsp (11 g) nutritional yeast

1 tbsp (8 g) soy lecithin granules

1½ tsp (8 g) sea salt

1 pt (340 g) blueberries

Lavender Syrup

2 cups (473 ml) filtered water

2 cups (453 g) food-safe lavender leaves and blossoms

1 cup (220 g) organic cane sugar (see Note)

Garnish

1 pt (340 g) blueberries

1 tbsp (4 g) food-safe lavender buds

For the lavender-blueberry layer, in a blender, combine all the lavender-blueberry ingredients and blend well until smooth. Taste and adjust with more maple syrup, salt and lemon juice, if desired. Pour the lavender-blueberry layer on top of the lemon layer. Place in the refrigerator and chill until the whole thing is firm, probably overnight to ensure that it sets up all the way to the center.

For the lavender syrup, bring the filtered water to a boil in a small saucepan. Add the lavender to the water and lower the heat to low. Simmer the lavender for 45 minutes, or until reduced by half. Add the cane sugar and simmer for another 15 minutes, or until the sugar is dissolved and the syrup easily coats the back of a spoon when dipped into the liquid. Use the lavender syrup to coat the fresh blueberries before using them for garnish. Drizzle more of the lavender syrup on top of each piece of cheesecake. Garnish with the lavender buds.

note Organic cane sugar is not a raw ingredient, so the lavender syrup is optional.

Chocolate-Raspberry Crepes

Some recipes are worth the work! These delicate crepe shells are stunning with the rich chocolate ganache and bright raspberries. You will be amazed at how well the avocado replaces dairy and eggs in the ganache. Young Thai coconuts are available in health food stores and Asian markets. They are white with pointy tops, and the water inside is delicious. You cut them open with a heavy knife (I strongly recommend you watch some videos online if you have never done this before), empty out the water/juice and then scoop out the fresh meat with a spoon. If you can't find the coconuts, then just replace with an equal amount of fresh banana.

Makes 10 crepes; serves 4 to 6

Crepe Shells

¼ cup (40 g) golden flaxseeds (brown flax is okay, but golden looks prettier)

½ cup (251 g) young Thai coconut meat

½ cup (118 ml) water

½ tsp salt

1 tbsp (30 ml) pure maple syrup

1 tsp ground cinnamon

1 banana

1 cup (64 g) hulled and sliced strawberries

Chocolate Ganache Filling

1½ small ripe avocados, pitted and peeled

2 tbsp (30 ml) melted coconut oil

¼ cup (60 ml) pure maple syrup

½ tsp vanilla extract

½ cup (55 g) raw cacao powder

For the crepe shells, in a dry blender, process the whole flaxseeds on high speed until finely ground. Remove from the blender and measure out ¼ cup (40 g) of ground flax. Put the measured ground flax back into the blender and add the remaining crepe shell ingredients. Puree until smooth, about 1 minute.

On a nonstick sheet (see Notes) spread the crepe batter into a thin layer and put into the dehydrator. You should get several trays of crepe batter, depending on the size of your dehydrator. If you have a small dehydrator, you can process the batter in batches. It will keep in your refrigerator for a few days. It may separate, and if this happens just blend it again in your blender. Dehydrate the crepe shells for 5 hours at 90°F (32°C).

After 5 hours, check them and see whether you can flip the nonstick sheet over and peel it away from the sheet of crepe batter. Carefully peel off the plastic and return the sheet of crepe batter to the dehydrator to finish drying another 3 to 5 hours at 90°F (32°C). The crepe should be flexible, so be careful not to overdry it, or it may become brittle. Remove the finished sheets of crepe batter from the dehydrator. Using a small plate or cup as a guide, cut out 3- to 5-inch (7.5- to 12.5-cm) rounds with a small knife. Wrap the finished shells in plastic wrap and place in your refrigerator. They will keep for several weeks stored in this way.

For the chocolate ganache filling, in a food processor, puree the avocado flesh until smooth. This will probably be too thick to process in a blender, so a food processor is recommended. Then, add the melted coconut oil, maple syrup and vanilla. Process until smooth. Finally, add the cacao powder and process until the chocolate is fully incorporated. Refrigerate for 2 to 6 hours, or until the mixture begins to set up enough to spread, almost a thick peanut butter consistency.

(continued)

Chocolate-Raspberry Crepes (continued)

Chocolate Sauce
½ cup (69 g) cashews

1 cup (236 ml) agave nectar or maple syrup

½ cup (55 g) raw cacao powder

1 tsp vanilla extract

½ cup (118 ml) water

Pinch of salt

½ tsp ground cinnamon

To Assemble
2 cups (250 g) raspberries

1 small bunch mint, for garnish

To make the chocolate sauce, add all of the sauce ingredients to a blender. Puree until smooth. Keep refrigerated. This will last up to 2 weeks.

To assemble the finished crepes, spread a few tablespoons of the chocolate ganache down the center of each of the 10 crepe shells. Place 4 raspberries on top of each ganache stripe. Roll the shell into a cylinder, using a little bit of the sticky ganache to help seal the roll overlap (this will help keep it from coming open). Assemble the crepes right before you are going to serve them, as the filling will start to make the crepe shells soggy if they sit for too long. Garnish with fresh mint.

notes: I recommend making this recipe only if you have a dehydrator! The crepes are pretty delicate and should be made at the lowest temperature possible. Although I recommend elsewhere using your oven as a dehydrator, I think it will be too hot, potentially making the crepes too crisp, and not sufficiently flexible.

When spreading out the crepe batter, you can use a nonstick sheet made for dehydrators, called Teflex, or you can wrap your dehydrator trays in plastic wrap.

Chocolate Gelato

Gelato made with avocado? Absolutely! The healthy fat contained in avocado makes for a supremely creamy dessert and pairs naturally with chocolate. The flavor of the avocado is undetectable, but the smooth texture shines through. If you like, you can fold chopped nuts, cacao nibs, granola or even fresh fruit into the mixture. When it is right out of the ice-cream maker, it's more of a soft-serve texture, but will harden up overnight. If you like it softer, just let it sit at room temperature for 5 to 10 minutes before serving.

Serves 4

Chocolate Gelato

1 cup (60 g) raw cacao powder

1 cup (138 g) cashews

1 small avocado

1 cup (236 ml) pure maple syrup, date syrup or agave nectar

1 cup (236 ml) water

2 tbsp (30 ml) melted coconut oil

1 tsp vanilla extract

¼ tsp sea salt

To Serve

½ cup (72 g) fresh blackberries or any other fresh fruit

¼ cup (30 g) Apple-Cinnamon Buckwheat Granola (page 18)

2 tbsp (30 ml) date syrup or pure maple syrup

In a blender, combine all the gelato ingredients and blend. When smooth and creamy, transfer to a bowl or lidded container and refrigerate for at least 1 hour (although you can chill the blended ice-cream base for 24 hours if desired). After the mixture is chilled, transfer it to an ice-cream maker and proceed according to the manufacturer's instructions. Place in the freezer after the ice-cream maker is done. Serve garnished with the blackberries, buckwheat granola and date syrup.

note If you don't have an ice-cream maker, you can make this gelato in your freezer. Simply place the gelato in a container, cover and place in your freezer. Allow to freeze overnight. Stirring a few times during the first 2 hours of freezing will help prevent ice crystals from forming. It will be grainier than if you make it in an ice-cream maker.

Mint Chocolate Chunk Gelato

I love using avocado as a base in vegan ice creams for the super-rich and creamy texture it gives. The thing I like most about it in this recipe is that the color of avocado works perfectly for the mint base, and the bright mint flavor is strong enough to mask any hint of avocado flavor.

Serves 10

Chocolate Chunks

¾ cup (177 ml) agave nectar or pure maple syrup

¾ cup (177 ml) coconut oil, melted

¼ tsp salt

¼ tsp vanilla extract

2 cups (200 g) raw cacao powder

Mint and Chocolate Gelato

2 cups (258 g) cashews

2 cups (473 ml) water

1 cup (236 ml) agave nectar, pure maple syrup, date syrup or rice syrup

1 small avocado, pitted and peeled

½ cup (48 g) fresh mint leaves

Pinch of salt

¼ cup (60 ml) melted coconut oil

1 tsp vanilla extract

To Serve

Fresh chopped mint leaves

Chocolate Sauce (page 160) (optional)

For the chocolate chunks, in a mixing bowl, combine the agave, melted coconut oil, salt and vanilla. Then, sift in the raw cacao powder and stir with a spatula until everything is well incorporated. Pour the mixture into a 9-inch (23-cm) square cake pan and refrigerate until hard, for 1 to 2 hours. Remove from the pan and chop into chunks however large and small you prefer. Keep this mixture refrigerated. This will stay good in your refrigerator for up to a month.

For the gelato, in an ice-cream maker, combine all the gelato ingredients and process according to the manufacturer's instructions. Fold in the chocolate chunks by hand, reserving some chunks for garnish, before putting the finished ice cream in the freezer.

To serve, scoop the gelato into a cup and garnish with the reserved chocolate chunks, chopped mint and chocolate sauce, if desired.

Lemon Crème Fraîche

with **Minted Berries** and **Maple**

A light dessert made with French style crème fraîche—made from young Thai coconut meat. This is another use for coconut yogurt, an extremely versatile ingredient. Another wonderful benefit: The healthy fats in the yogurt will make your skin glow.

Serves 2

Lemon Crème Fraîche
1 cup (236 ml) Coconut Yogurt (page 30)

3 tbsp (45 ml) pure maple syrup

1 tsp grated lemon zest

Minted Berries
4 cups (150 g) mixed berries, such as blueberries, strawberries, raspberries and blackberries

4 sprigs mint, for garnish

For the crème fraîche, place the coconut yogurt in a bowl. Add the maple syrup and lemon zest and whisk well to combine. Cover with plastic wrap and refrigerate until very cold, 1 hour or longer.

For the minted berries, rinse the berries and gently pat dry. If using strawberries, rinse first, then hull and halve (or quarter, if large) lengthwise. Place the mixed berries in a large bowl and gently toss to combine.

Divide the berries among 2 dessert bowls. Place a dollop of about ¼ cup (60 ml) of the crème fraîche in the middle of the berries and garnish each with a mint sprig.

> note: The Lemon Crème Fraîche can be prepared 2 days ahead; keep covered and refrigerated.

Apple Cobbler Sundae

with **Walnut-Date Crumble**

Cobbler is one of the easiest desserts to throw together and so delicious in its simplicity. You can make this refreshing and healthy dessert with a wide variety of fruits. Try peaches in the summer or a mango-berry combination. Young strawberries, straight from the farmers' market, with a hint of balsamic glaze are a great option, too.

Serves 2 to 4

Crumble Topping

1 cup (114 g) walnuts

1 tsp ground cinnamon

Pinch of salt

1 tsp vanilla extract

3 dates, pitted and chopped roughly

Filling

3 sweet red apples (such as Fuji or Gala)

2 tbsp (30 ml) pure maple syrup

1 tsp ground cinnamon

⅛ tsp ground cardamom

½ cup (75 g) raisins

1 tsp vanilla extract

Pinch of salt

To Serve

1 pt (285 g) vegan vanilla ice cream (I used coconut milk ice cream), or 5 oz (140 g) coconut whipped cream

Date syrup or maple syrup, for drizzling on top

For the crumble topping, in a food processor, combine the walnuts, cinnamon, salt and vanilla. Pulse until roughly broken up. Distribute the dates evenly over the walnut mixture. Pulse a few more times until the dates and nuts are well mixed but still have nice big pieces. Set aside until ready to use. This mixture will keep for weeks in an airtight container in your refrigerator or freezer.

For the filling, cut the apples into a small dice. Transfer to a mixing bowl along with the maple syrup, cinnamon, cardamom, raisins, vanilla and salt. Toss well and allow to marinate 1 hour or up to 24 hours.

To assemble the apple cobbler sundae, spoon the filling into 2 or 4 bowls or parfait cups. Sprinkle a generous amount of cobbler topping onto the apple filling, serve with vegan vanilla ice cream or coconut whipped cream and drizzle with the date syrup.

> note If you have a dehydrator, place the marinated fruit on a tray and dehydrate for an hour at 118°F (48°C) to make it especially tender! If you are just marinating on your countertop, don't worry. It will be a little crisper than if it has a little time in the dehydrator.

Cherry-Chocolate Ganache Tart

If you have never tried chocolate and avocado paired together, you are in for a real treat. Avocado has a naturally creamy texture that is a perfect replacement for dairy products in rich desserts, and the chocolate transforms the color of the avocados to look exactly like traditional ganache. Don't tell your friends and family what the secret ingredient is and see whether they can guess. This dessert freezes beautifully if you're worried about making too much—you can actually eat it right out of the freezer and it's perfect. Just make sure you're not freezing the fruit topping, only the chocolate tart base.

Serves 4

Crust

1 cup (114 g) walnuts

½ cup (83 g) chopped dried Bing cherries (unsweetened and unsulfured, if possible)

Pinch of salt

1 tsp ground cinnamon

1 tbsp (15 ml) water (if needed)

Chocolate Filling

1 small avocado, pitted and peeled

4 tbsp (60 ml) melted coconut oil

½ cup (118 ml) pure maple syrup

½ cup (40 g) raw cacao powder

½ tsp vanilla extract

¼ tsp sea salt

1 tbsp (8 g) soy lecithin granules

Cherry Topping

2 cups (310 g) fresh or frozen cherries, pitted

1 tbsp (15 ml) pure maple syrup

Pinch of sea salt

Line 4 mini tart pans or cupcake pan wells with plastic wrap before making the tarts so the crust releases easily once it's set. For the crust, in a food processor, pulse the walnuts until they are broken up into small pieces. Add the cherries, salt and cinnamon. Pulse until the cherries are well incorporated and the mixture begins to stick together. Add the water if the mixture will not stick together when pressed firmly in your hand. You should be able to form a ball of the crust mixture. Press firmly and evenly into the prepared pans. Set the pans aside until ready to add the filling.

For the filling, in a food processor, combine the avocado with the coconut oil and maple syrup. Process until smooth, without any chunks. Add the cacao powder, vanilla, salt and soy lecithin and process until smooth. Pour into the prepared crusts. Refrigerate overnight to set up.

To make the cherry topping, toss the cherries with the maple syrup and salt until well coated. When you're ready to serve the tarts, remove from the molds, place on plates and top with the cherry topping.

note You can use any dried fruit for the crust. Dates work especially well if you don't have access to dried cherries.

Chocolate Truffles

with **Gooey Date Centers**

Creamy dark chocolate with a perfect salted caramel center—you'd never guess they're vegan! These tempting truffles make welcome gifts as well. Just make sure to store them in the refrigerator.

Makes 24 to 30 pieces

Caramel Filling

40 soft Medjool dates, pitted

4 tsp (20 ml) vanilla extract

2 tsp (10 g) fine sea salt

4 tbsp (60 ml) melted coconut oil

½ cup (125 g) natural pure almond butter

½ cup (118 ml) pure maple syrup

Chocolate Coating

16 oz (453 g) vegan dark baking chocolate

Garnish

1 tbsp (18 g) coarse sea salt (I used Maldon sea salt flakes)

Prepare a pan (I used a mini bread pan 3 x 6 inches [4.5 x 15 cm]) by lining the inside completely in plastic wrap. Make sure the plastic wrap comes up over the sides.

For the filling, in a food processor, combine all the caramel filling ingredients and process until completely smooth. Depending on the size of your food processor, you will probably need to process this recipe in two batches. When the mixture is smooth, press it evenly into the bottom of the prepared pan and place in the freezer for about 2 hours. There might be some liquid pooling around the top of the caramel—this is a mixture of coconut oil and maple syrup. Turn the pan upside down and drain out the excess liquid so it doesn't pool up too much when you chill the caramel.

For the chocolate coating, melt the chocolate in the top of a double boiler set over gently boiling water (make sure the water does not touch the top pan). If you don't have a double boiler, fill a medium saucepan with water and bring it to a boil. Then, place the chocolate in a heatproof mixing bowl over the saucepan and balance it on top of the saucepan. Whisk the chocolate frequently as it melts.

Place the melted chocolate in a medium mixing bowl right before you are ready to coat the caramel. Make sure that you don't let it cool too much. Line a baking sheet with parchment paper.

Remove the caramel filling from the freezer and release it from the pan. Working quickly, cut the caramel with a sharp knife into your desired shapes. Dip each piece into the chocolate (see Note) and coat thoroughly. You want to let any excess chocolate drain off the caramel piece over the bowl before placing them on the prepared baking sheet.

Finally, after they have been placed on the baking sheet and the chocolate is still soft, use a fork to gently touch the top of each chocolate to create a pretty pattern of lines. Sprinkle them with Maldon salt flakes, and place in the refrigerator to chill. Store in the refrigerator in a closed container for up to 2 weeks, if they last that long.

note: It is important to work quickly and gently with the caramels when you're dipping them in the chocolate. You want them to keep their shape with a nice smooth chocolate covering over the caramel center. I like to use two forks to gently lift the caramels out of the chocolate and transfer them to the parchment-lined baking sheet. If you touch them too frequently with your hands, they will start to lose their shape due to the heat of your skin.

Pumpkin Pie

with Mission Fig Crust

Pumpkin pie is one of those desserts that translates especially well to raw vegan cuisine and is a fabulous option to bring to a holiday get-together. Try this with a vegan whipped cream.

Serves 6

Fig Walnut Crust

2 cups (250 g) raw walnuts

1 tsp ground cinnamon

¼ tsp salt

12 dried Mission figs, stemmed and soaked for 20 minutes in filtered water

Pumpkin Filling

2 cups (250 g) raw cashews, soaked in water, then drained and rinsed

2 cups (250 g) seeded, peeled and chopped raw pumpkin (see Notes)

1 cup (236 ml) melted coconut oil

2 tbsp (16 g) nutritional yeast (optional; see Notes)

½ cup (118 ml) pure maple syrup

1 tsp fresh lemon juice

2 tbsp (11 g) pumpkin pie spice

2 tbsp (8 g) soy lecithin granules (see Notes)

¼ tsp salt

To Serve

Coconut whipped cream (optional)

For the crust, in a food processor, combine the walnuts, cinnamon and salt and pulse until the nuts are pretty broken up. Drain the figs and add them whole to the food processor. Pulse some more until the mixture begins to stick together and the figs are fully incorporated. Remove from the food processor and press into the bottom of a 9-inch (23-cm) pie pan. Lining the pan in plastic makes the pie easier to remove. Press down on the mixture well to make sure that the crust is firm. Set aside.

For the pie filling, in a blender, combine all the filling ingredients and puree until smooth. Pour into the prepared crust and smooth the top with a spatula. Refrigerate the pie overnight and serve topped with coconut whipped cream, if desired.

notes Raw pumpkin can be very difficult to work with, especially when it comes to peeling and seeding it. You can substitute raw, peeled butternut squash or even peeled and chopped carrots if you find the pumpkin too challenging. Alternatively, you can use canned pure pumpkin puree.

The nutritional yeast is added to help give the pie a cheesecake flavor, but feel free to omit!

Soy lecithin granules are available in the supplement section of your local health food store. They are used to help the pie set, and I don't recommend skipping this ingredient. The pie will not hold together as well. The leftover lecithin (and you will have some!) is a great addition to smoothies for brain function and joint health. Be sure to purchase non-GMO lecithin!

Chocolate Brownies

Rich and chocolaty, these brownies also double as a healthy snack on the go. Feel free to reduce the sweetener or add protein powder to the mixture if you would like to use it as a power boost. Maca is an ingredient added for additional nutrition, but is completely optional. It's a root vegetable from South America that is known for helping to regulate blood sugar, increase energy and balance hormones. It has a neutral flavor and pairs nicely with cacao. A little really goes a long way! It's a completely optional ingredient, so don't worry about omitting it, if necessary.

Makes 24 brownies

4 cups (500 g) walnut pieces

4 cups (500 g) pecan pieces

2 cups (294 g) pitted and chopped dates

1 cup (80 g) raw cacao powder

½ cup (118 ml) agave nectar or pure maple syrup

2 tbsp (40 g) maca powder (optional)

1 banana, peeled and chopped

1 tsp vanilla extract

Zest of 1 orange

Pinch of salt

Soak the walnuts, pecans and dates together in water to cover for 1 to 2 hours. Drain in a colander when ready to use. Discard the water. Place this mixture in a food processor and add the cacao powder, agave, maca powder (if using), banana, vanilla, orange zest and salt. Puree until smooth. If you have a small food processor, you may have to work in batches and mix everything together in a bowl at the end. You really do need to make this recipe in a processor, as it's too thick to make in a blender. Using a spatula, spread out the batter on a solid dehydrator sheet (see Notes), ½ inch (1.3 cm) thick, and dehydrate for 8 hours at 118°F (48°C). Flip once and dehydrate for another 8 hours. I usually cut the brownies at the end to get the size I want.

notes A hint for flipping the brownies safely is to put another dehydrator tray on top of the brownies, sandwiching the sheet of brownies. Flip the trays together and then carefully remove the solid sheet from the brownies and return them to the dehydrator to finish them.

This recipe can also be made in your oven if you don't have a dehydrator. Just spread the brownies on a parchment paper–lined cookie sheet instead of a dehydrator sheet and place them in an oven set at its lowest temperature. Crack the door of the oven open about 1 inch (2.5 cm) to allow the moisture to escape. If you use your oven, the cooking time will be shorter, so check the brownies every hour or less to make sure they aren't drying out too much.

If you don't have solid dehydrator sheets, you can spread the brownie mixture on parchment paper or wrap your dehydrator sheets in plastic wrap.

Tiramisu

with Cashew Mascarpone

Lightly sweet, exceptionally creamy with a hint of coffee. A perfectly divine end to a healthy meal!

Makes one 9-inch (23-cm) cake; serves 8 to 12

Mascarpone Cream Layer
1 cup (137 g) young Thai coconut meat

¼ cup (60 ml) water

¼ cup (60 ml) light agave nectar

1½ tsp (8 ml) vanilla extract

¼ cup (60 ml) unfiltered, melted extra virgin coconut oil

1 tbsp (8 g) soy lecithin granules

Espresso Mixture
1 tbsp (15 ml) pure maple syrup

¼ cup (60 ml) cold-brewed espresso

1 tbsp (15 ml) water

Cake Layer
2 cups (296 g) almond meal or almond flour

1½ cups (222 g) coconut flour

3 cups (450 g) pitted and roughly chopped dates

1 tbsp (15 ml) pure maple syrup

1 tbsp (15 ml) vanilla extract

Raw cacao powder, for garnish

For the mascarpone layer, in a blender, combine all the mascarpone ingredients and blend well until smooth. Pour into a mixing bowl and refrigerate for at least 1 hour. After the mixture has chilled, whip by hand with a whisk or in a stand mixer. Set aside until ready to assemble the tiramisu.

For the espresso mixture, in a bowl, whisk together the maple syrup, espresso and water. Set aside.

For the cake layer, in a food processor, combine all the cake layer ingredients. Pulse until the mixture is well mixed and crumbly.

To assemble the tiramisu, press half of cake layer mix firmly into the bottom of an 8-inch (20.5-cm) springform or round cake pan. Pour half of the espresso mixture on top.

Spread a thin layer of the mascarpone cream on top of the cake layer. Place the pan in the freezer and allow the mascarpone to freeze all the way through. Remove from the freezer and gently press the reserved cake mixture on top of the frozen mascarpone cream. Pour the reserved espresso mixture on top of the final cake layer. Dust the top with raw cacao powder. Allow to chill overnight in your refrigerator before serving.

> *note* The mascarpone cream gets frozen before the second layer of cake is pressed onto it, because it is too soft otherwise. Do not skip this step, or your tiramisu will not be as pretty.

Acknowledgments

First and foremost, I would like to thank everyone at Page Street Publishing Co. for making this book possible and for being incredible collaborators. This project has been a dream of mine for a long time, and it would not be possible without all the amazing people at Page Street.

I would like to express my deepest gratitude to all the people who have supported me over the years, including all the people who have eaten my food and encouraged me to keep cooking! But there are a few people I would like to thank especially.

My mother, Judy Johnston, for all her help in putting together this book and for teaching me to love healthy food from a young age.

My father, Brian Carr, and his partner, Meg Selig, for their love and support.

Beto, for trying all my food and giving me honest feedback and encouragement.

My friends Dawn Weisberg and Kristan Andrews, for walking the raw vegan path with me and sharing recipes, ideas and support. Thank you for believing in me!

I would like to thank Nikki Sharp, Chloe Coscarelli and Ron Russell for honoring me with their endorsements.

Thank you to everyone who has eaten my food and supported my journey as a chef.

Rachel Carr is a raw vegan chef based in Los Angeles, California. She holds an MFA in theater design from New York University, and prior to becoming a chef, worked as a costume designer in New York and L.A. After moving to L.A. in 2002, she was introduced to raw veganism and immediately fell in love with the fresh, vibrant flavors, health benefits and increased energy she experienced and hasn't looked back. She began her journey as a raw vegan chef in 2006, when she switched careers to pursue helping others heal their lives through food.

Rachel is the force behind many unique plant-based restaurants in the United States and is a prolific chef, food writer and cooking instructor. She began her career as executive chef of Cru, a raw vegan bistro in Los Angeles known for its refined and innovative high raw cuisine. Rachel went on to open Six Main, a farm-to-table plant-based restaurant in Connecticut, and Chavela, a vegan Peruvian sangria bar in the Hollywood neighborhood of Los Angeles. She has also worked as the head chef at such well-known plant-based restaurants as Sun Café and Wanderlust Café in Los Angeles.

Currently, Rachel is working as executive chef for the Pizza Plant, a new plant-based pizza concept. She loves to teach others the art of plant-based cooking and hopes to encourage readers to take charge of their health and well-being. When she isn't in the kitchen, she relaxes by hiking, practicing yoga and checking out local farmers' markets.

Index